86,400

SECONDS A DAY

Manage Your Time Down to the Second
to be Productive and Profitable

P. K. POTEAU, PH.D.

86,400 Seconds A Day: Manage Your Time Down to the Second to be Productive and Profitable
Copyright © 2021 P. K. Poteau, Ph.D.
Publisher: Pierre Poteau Books, www.pkpoteau.com

ISBN-9781710090628
ISBN-9781087825960
ISBN & EBOOK-978-1-0878-5320-8
Library of Congress Control Number-1-8185030531

Disclaimer: This book is meant to be a source of valuable information for readers interested in self-improvement. It is not meant as a substitute for the quality of direct expert assistance of therapists, counselors, or coaches.

I dedicate this book to my children,
Kensky and Ashley.

The future is so bright before both of you.

Always involve God first in whatever you do,
and everything else will fall into place.

Always be thankful for what you have

Always have a goal.
Your goals are your reasons to live.

Always honor your dreams.
They are your reasons to live.

*Leadership wins your heart and soul;
good management keeps you in constant motion.*

– P. K. Poteau, Ph.D.

Contents

Contents

Contents

Preface

As I sit here, rain pours against my window. The day grows old as I reflect on the many things about this book that I had hoped to accomplish and put into words. I looked deep within to ensure this book would be the right thing to do. There were things I wanted to share, and I felt I had something to say. I realized there was something I could offer—something that would matter to the rest of humanity in the world.

I knew in the beginning it would be an endeavor, but it was my dream to see my words, my story, and my experience—all on the written page. Long before I ever dreamed of writing this book, I could see it being written; a story about to unfold. There was a seed firmly planted when I was a young, full-time soldier who was leading troops safely through two tours in Iraq. In doing so, I used my time management skills and goal setting to impact my life—and many other lives. Over the years, my practical use of time management improved my life and continued to lead me to remain productive and garner great successes. My skills allowed me to complete my schooling and earn multiple degrees, a successful job, an incredible family, excellent health, and staying active over the years through routine workouts and exercise.

I have always been a person who thrives on helping people, and helping you is at the heart of this book. I want to help people who believe they don't have the time or understanding to improve their lives. I desire to reassure people they have the drive and passion within them and remind them that the key is to dig a little deeper and make time—to improve their lives.

My life has been a journey of many challenges, and over the years, God has shown me that we are all equal in many ways. The one ultimate fact declaring equality for all is that we each only have 86,400 seconds in a day. This fact is an equal share from God to everyone—no less and no more. What we do with our time is essential in experiencing a prosperous life. Knowing this fact, I have written this book to share my organizational skills to help as many people as possible make the best of each day. I feel in my heart this is a rare opportunity and a profound responsibility to help others live the best life possible.

In this book, I share the exact methods of how I accomplished goals in my life. I explain how I went from being a private in the U.S. Army, with three college credit hours, to becoming a captain, and earning both an MBA and a Ph.D. I did all of this despite the adversities and immense obligations surrounding me in my life. I worked diligently and faced challenges to improve my experience and keep pushing forward. My work was completed with the best intentions, interest, and a solemn duty to myself and my family to get things accomplished. The one message I want you to comprehend fully is this: You can do anything you set your mind to do. I want to show you that if I can do it—you can do it, too.

So, I want you to settle in and take a deep breath. Take your time with my words. Explore the possibilities because within these pages are the methods and plans to educate you on how to change your life for the better. You will soon know that you can accomplish anything and everything through the best use of your time and time management. You will discover a new superpower by prioritizing and eliminating distractions to avoid procrastination, which leads to a stagnant and unfulfilled life. My wish is for you to use your mind to discover your possibilities, abilities, to know your heart—and most of all—to know who you are.

Introduction

Here you are. The project in front of you is idyllic, with the potential to be ideal. You are inspired. The project's energy thrives in you. You are ready, and the project seems to be the perfect opportunity to reach success.

The key is to not let time slip through your hands.

Time has a way of disappearing quickly.

Management of your time is the catalyst between starting a project or coming to a grinding halt. Everyone on the planet has 86,400 seconds a day. How you use these seconds to better your life is up to you and your choices.

From my extensive career in the military, starting as a private, the being promoted to an officer, and eventually obtaining a leadership management role, I acknowledged the importance of time management as the direct method in making use of every second. Time management is an indispensable aspect of obtainable goal setting, achieving consistency in carrying out a plan to meet the goal, and working with mastery to full completion.

This book, *86,400 Seconds a Day* addresses issues of time management, goal setting, and facing tasks that move you forward to completion. I've poured my heart into writing this manual to assist you in restructuring your life for true time efficiency. I've taken my vast experience, my successes, and my failures, and used them as the foundation for real-world time management.

This book sets the tone and brings increased value and structure as a time management formula. By learning the importance of making each second count, my hope is this book becomes a helpful guide in discovering unlimited flow and positive change in your life.

From my experience as a military officer to my academic career, I offer real-life methods that let you tackle the enormity of every task in all aspects of your life—from work to play and the many tasks in between. This book was written for every person, from any walk of life. You are the sole reason for writing this book. I want you to reach your goals because I've seen how proper management of time has saved people from desperation and failure. By adjusting your perception and keeping a positive attitude shift toward management of your time, you will be rewarded with unlimited potential and future success. The smallest of efforts toward a commitment to respect the flow of time can alter your thought process and unlock your vast potential.

You'll find value in this book that you may personalize and use. My goal for you as you read is that you'll take an honest assessment of how you use time and understand the matter of time management. I want you to finish reading this book and have a clear understanding of how you are responsible for your time.

The responsibility is in your hands.

People achieve goals through growing into an understanding of how to use time. It is an important lesson that you must learn on your own. As you learn, I want your self-esteem to escalate as you experience personal and professional satisfaction and achieve a level of financial success that matches the desire you have for living life as you want it to be.

The recognition of the use of time in your day will revolutionize your life. It opens opportunities and awakens you to the moment's potential. Seeing how you are able to generate extra time, combat distractions, and reprogram old habits to form new, better ones is within these pages. You can find the right formula for increased production and healthy coping strategies all while obtaining a satisfying balance, or loop, between work and relaxation. I hope and pray you'll learn to use your own 86,400 seconds every day of your life to live a fruitful, healthy, and prosperous life—the best life, the life you deserve.

Sincerely,
P. K. Poteau, Ph.D.

Chapter I
The Importance and Benefits of Goal Setting

You already know it is good to set goals. There are many goals you've set and reached, and it's likely you've set goals that were partly reached, never reached, or forgotten. How were you taught to set your goals? What would you like to learn now about how to set and reach goals?

Exactly What is Goal Setting?

'Goal setting' is a phrase that is used quite often, and in my experience, it is not given proper importance in business and life. Not achieving goals is directly related to disappointment from excessive expectations of the outcome of any project. Your ability or inability to weigh a project with lofty expectations is directly correlated to getting tasks accomplished or not. Goals are tasks associated with the time you set and are based on the conclusions you induce as visualized outcomes. By expecting definitive results, you set yourself up for failure. When it comes to time management and goals, many people are guilty of getting in the way of themselves and preventing goals from being met.

I encourage the practical use of time and goal setting. I present the best emphasis and importance of setting obtainable goals. I will share my acquired knowledge of business and how it relates to career success through specific strategies and anecdotal evidence I've gleaned through my journey of distinct life accomplishments.

My entire life has been spent following a path of attainable goals—but some were not-so-attainable. It was my good fortune to live an idyllic life in a normal American family. I was the eldest of three brothers and, along with my mom and dad, all of us encountered struggles. My brothers and I made the best of them by setting friendly, brotherly goals and initiating them as challenges through a friendly competition to reach each one of them. Each of us would set a goal to obtain and put an "execution milestone plan" in place. As kids, our goals were simple: getting through elementary school, making good grades, and making the honors list in junior high school.

These goals were competitive and pushed each of us toward achieving and setting higher attainable goals. Our mutual goal setting got us each through high school, then college, and on to obtaining masters and doctorate degrees.

We were playful and fierce as we went out for each other to push and achieve those goals as young students. Each of us at turns made the goals harder and more challenging then we strived to push each other further and further. Doing our best was fuel for our goals. After we achieved each goal, we would set the bar higher and build in increased specifics for what each of us set out to do. Each of us went after our goals in direct ways as we moved forward in increments until we achieved success. It seemed we brothers were on a task-and-goal marathon.

What I learned from my brothers is that goals are accomplished one at a time by sharpening a sense of hyper-focus. This means that every step of the way must be planned for and defined. To say it was easy would be an untruth. It wasn't. But, if I had not learned to set and manage my goals, I would not be where I am today. I am here to share my experience to aid you in moving your career, life, and/or business forward as you fulfill every goal you want to achieve.

To get started you must know the technical aspects of time management and the definition of effective goal setting. I base the technical descriptions upon a goal-setting theory that addresses the process and the effects of tasks being performed and accomplished through setting specific goals. It has been proven throughout the years that setting specific, attainable, and focused goals are achieved better than broad, less accessible, and lofty types of goals.

Edwin Locke, a researcher, published a scientific paper in 1968 titled, "Toward a Theory of Task Motivation and Incentive." The paper included Locke's groundbreaking Goal Setting Theory. It was an authentic glimpse and blueprint of businesses, big or small, that showed the correlation between goal setting and productivity, and employee engagement. Locke's goal setting theory addressed the idea that setting goals with strategic productivity methods motivated completion of the goal. He concluded that employee engagement was both clear and actionable when outcomes were proved to be achievable.

Locke's work showed me that any workplace challenge is not a bad thing if the goal can be defined and given steps for follow-through. Once I determine a goal and gather the specifics, it aids me in gaining a vision of the result. The real way to establish a goal is to support it with practical action steps. Here are the action steps and principles to follow to make your goals achievable:

Clarity. The clarity of a goal is determined by how clear, measurable, and achievable the original idea is. A specific goal is attainable by setting a timeline for completion.

Challenge. Any goal worth pursuing must present a degree of difficulty in maintaining motivation. When a goal is presented as a challenge, it will push you to strive harder to achieve that goal.

Commitment. A high level of commitment must be put forth to achieve any goal. Hold yourself accountable by being deliberate in meeting your goals. Find an accountability partner and share the steps you take on the way to it in order to stay on track.

Feedback. Set yourself up to respond and be open to feedback on your pathway to achieving your goal. If, along the way, you find the goal was too lofty to attain, it is best to adjust the goal midway than to quit and not hit your goal.

Task complexity. Be open to the difficulty of the task you have set forth. This is vital. If a goal you have set is complicated, give yourself leniency in the learning curve time frame. If the goal is discovered to be too tough to attain, then adjust, and give yourself time to allow for the best chance in succeeding.

Purpose of Setting Goals

The way I set my goals with my brothers is a conclusive example of the positive effects of having a definitive plan for your life and how planning is essential in hitting your goals. The key to increasing your advantage and chances of achieving your goals is to define and write down your goals. Having a record of what you want to accomplish in front of you holds you accountable to yourself. Specifying what you're passionate about and writing the plan out in front of you is the key to finding success. Consider these general questions:

Where do I start?
What are the things I hope to do?
What do I most want to achieve?

Then, you resist the temptation to answer, "I don't know." The thing is—you do know. And, for some reason, you resist finding what you know. Maybe someone once let you believe that you didn't have a certain talent, ability, knack, or passion. Maybe you were groomed to grow up and be something that you really did not want to be. Whatever the reason, you have to find a way to discover the truth you've kept in lockdown.

When making important life decisions, it is imperative to be honest and forthcoming with yourself. Don't worry about others and their opinions. You must do what makes you happy, and the rest will fall into place. Once you discover the passion in your life, you can use it to drive the rest of your life toward success.

Most people do not understand how to take the time to set goals, nor do they even do it. They do not see the value in it and get used to life controlling them instead of being in control of their own lives. Although discovering your passion can be challenging, it should be the main priority because, without it, you will float aimlessly without direction. Let's look at some of the best reasons to set goals for your life.

Setting Yourself up For Success

Each of us has the exact amount of time every day of our lives. No more and no less. From the moment you wake up to the time you rest your head, it is up to you to guide what happens to make your life move forward. Having your goals prioritized will set you up for positive outcomes—and great success.

When you do not place your goals as a top priority, you lose out on immense opportunities, which could prove to have dramatic effects on your life. Diligently working toward your goals will put you in an incredible position to see massive success in whatever you choose to do.

Having Goals Helps You Define What is Important

Having your goals set will reveal what is truly important in your life. Through your efforts, you will discover who you are and the essential people around you. You will find the meaning of family, work, school, and relationships—and all will start to have a profound purpose.

When you don't go through the process of defining goals in your life, you could begin to feel broken, unfocused, and even experience failure in other efforts in life.

Experience the Joy in Living

Pursuing your dreams by setting long- and short-term goals will give you a roadmap to achieve success. The only thing stopping you is when you do nothing. Achieving your goals brings a deep satisfaction that is hard to describe. The feeling of accomplishment can bring joy to every aspect of your life. Everything around you will begin to make sense. This joy goes a long way and begins to affect everyone around you in positive ways.

Your achievements help your family and friends to see you as strong, capable, and able. Having your family and friends in your corner, believing in you, and supporting you brings great happiness and joy to your life.

Goals are a Roadmap

By setting your goals, you give yourself a pathway to freedom and success. The secret is to draw a line in the sand and pinpoint the main goal you want to achieve. Make this goal your life's destination.

Most people do not have a destination in their life. They wander and float through life without meaning or direction. Without the destination, you will veer off your path—and run the risk of never reaching your goals.

Use your goals as a compass to direct your life and use your passion to push you to grasp what it is you intend to achieve. The only way to do this is by treating your goals as a top priority and taking these aggressive actions will shape and direct everything in your life.

Goals Bring Hope and Confidence

Following your passions is fulfilling in every way imaginable. When you follow ambitions, your immense effort morphs into a greater sense of dedication and direction within yourself.

Goals are your dreams! Goals exist to instill a sense of confidence and, most of all, hope for your future.

How to Avoid Distractions and Stay Focused

I spent eight years in the Armed Forces serving as a chemical and operations officer, and six years as an enlisted member. I needed to become adept at working with technology during my years in the military in Iraq. My job relied on time management and leadership, which required me to maintain stringent focus at all times. I discovered during those years that staying on track with my tasks by alleviating distractions was crucial to accomplishing any goal at hand. The reality was and is this: with technology comes significant distraction.

Distraction!

You can't escape it because technology is a double-edged sword. The convenience technology affords for many of today's jobs makes possible that which was not possible not that long ago. And with that convenience comes the propensity to become distracted as it introduces complexity at many levels, which adds to the work. Recapturing and generating focus are a challenge and accomplishment in these modern days of work.

What are the Distractions?

The reality is this: I'm sitting here working to write this book. I'm typing on this computer and to the left of me is a mobile phone where the world is at my fingertips. The urge to "hop on" and check emails, look at the sports scores, and check social media is powerful.

These types of distractions are not exactly clear. They appear to be a part of normal life—people accept them as routine and not distractions. New information is available and there for the taking—it makes you feel like you have a responsibility to it, that you need it. It cannot be ignored!

The truth is—you must ignore it. It is less important than what you need to do to meet your goals.

To maintain the level of productivity to hit your goals, recognizing and reducing your distractions is vital. Have you examined how much time you spend on nonproductive things, leaving your tasks to be delayed or not completed at all? Probably not, because distraction is difficult to measure—unless you realize that you've been doing something else and two hours have passed.

To eliminate anything in your life that could be a possible distraction problem, the best route is to determine what the real distractions are. Anything in your world that can take your attention away from the goal at hand could be labeled your "Achilles heel" for getting things done.

What are the distractions in your life? Let's examine some common ones so you can see how they make you a victim.

Technology
Computer
Cell Phone
Laptop
Tablet
Smart Watch

TV/Radio

Social Media Outlets
 Facebook
 Twitter
 LinkedIn
 Instagram
 Pinterest
 YouTube
 Tik Tok

Environment
 Family Members
 Co-workers
 Neighbors / Friends
 Events

Removing the urge to concentrate on anything other than the task at hand is easier said than done. Social media is a leading cause of distraction today. The curiosity generated with social media is on a different scale when it comes to distractions in the day—these distractions are mental escapism. Social media sites, the email inbox, even grabbing an extra cup of coffee, clutter your mind instead of clearing it for working complexity. The need to reward your brain amidst the hustle of everyday tasks becomes overwhelming. Your brain works overtime in convincing you to stay motivated, and you feel you need a reward to keep going.

Projects, big or small, with all the pressure involved with deadlines and dates due, require you to fill a different set of needs. The fixation on social media curiosity, for example, is caused by a chemical in your brain. Much like being addicted to cigarettes, drugs, and even food, when you don't have it, your brain releases chemicals telling you that you must get it. Dopamine is the chemical released that creates the good feelings you may get when you connect with social media. The feelings of happiness, satisfaction, and euphoria you experience when viewing or reading social media create strong emotions and sensations that soon make your brain crave more.

The urge to check social media can be labeled as a real addiction, and this addiction is at mass proportion in our society. It is challenging to resist the urge to check social media. It is challenging to resist partaking in other distractions. Sometimes, the urge is more than you can bear or handle and morphs into an addiction. This addiction leads to wasting an immense amount of time and not achieving goals.

Your Brain and Science

Is your brain perhaps in the wrong place at the right time? In looking at it from a scientific standpoint, the Ventral Tegmental Area (VTA) of the brain is the section that craves the dopamine released when you log into social media. This is the area of the brain that demands and needs more dopamine and recognizes the deficiency when you don't have a social media connection. And this works to trigger the "crave" to get on and check it out, causing major distractions when you don't need or want to be distracted. The brain's VTA portion is the culprit of significant distraction, and with social media, it is not your friend.

There are specific things and solutions you can do to escape the trap and cycle of distraction:

Working in isolation

Silencing your phone

Journaling

Taking breaks

Getting a good night's rest

Having a clean work area

Isolation

For starters, working in isolation by getting away from everyone to a place of comfort is ideal. In today's world, it may be challenging to find a place of solitude away from everyone. Everything from an office cubicle and piles of paper to kids and family responsibilities, becoming centered and free from distractions, is a difficult task. The goal of achieving isolation, in most instances, is to find silence and solitude. An environment free of noise with a peaceful setting is an optimal setup for consistent concentration.

From the time you open your eyes to the time your head hits the pillow you are inundated with noise pollution. Sounds such as notifications from email, social media, text messaging, and the old-fashioned ringing phone are massive distractions that happen hundreds of times a day.

Quiet time alone to reflect should be scheduled. Make it a priority and set a time for yourself to find a space to be alone and away from all distractions. One way to combat the urge to check social media and other distractions is to monitor the time you spend on all technology. Discipline yourself by keeping notes on time spent online and on social media—or pay attention to the notices you get regarding time spent on your computer or cell phone. Please keep a record of the time and allow yourself only dedicated blocks of time and stick to it. You will find that by tracking your social media exploration, you will spend less time off task and more time working toward your tasks at hand.

Make the most of the quiet times you set for yourself in isolation. Work to focus on relaxation and quieting your mind during these sessions. Find the best place and time that works for you. Everyone is different, and what works for you might not work for others. Some people are more focused in the morning, while other people find themselves focused at night. Mid-afternoon is a time when some people are the most creative. I have even heard that some people are most innovative in the car while driving or on the bus going to and from work. I've talked to people who say their creative ideas come through and flow after they've exercised, even though they are fatigued.

The key is to understand your body and your mind. Test what works best for you and use that quiet alone time to produce ideas. Let it flow. Get to know your biorhythmic work style and stick to a time and place where distraction is not likely to occur. Find your time and place away from noise and people and allow this time to take precedence in your life.

Journaling

You'll be able to do your journaling after setting up a space for isolation and being in silence. Clarity in thought is achieved primarily by organizing your thoughts to achieve your goals—and you must be able to "hear" your thoughts. Take advantage of achieving clarity of mind by keeping a personal journal. Journaling during your quiet time allows you to achieve a stream-of-consciousness where thoughts you didn't even know existed can come through. These are the thoughts that can reorganize your mind. Journaling generates ideas and assists you in creating your next steps with the goals you want to achieve.

There is great value in stream-of-consciousness writing. Study how to do this in the best way that works for you. Some people close their eyes for a few minutes while focusing on breathing. Some light a candle and watch the flame until they reach an appropriate state of relaxation. Others feel ready to write only when they have the best pen, or blank (as opposed to unlined) paper. Some people write outlines, others write sentences, some write inside bubbles; others write lists and some draw before they write, making illustrations and then giving them captions. There are journals that include writing prompts to open your mind and let you start writing by answering a question or stating a thought.

There is no wrong way to journal. Making lists, defining distractions, and writing about both essential and unessential tasks help you re-shuffle the residue that clogs your mind and hinders your ability to achieve your goals. Journaling is a way to gain personal insight, increase awareness, and refine your vocabulary. Capturing your feelings in words leads to enhanced growth of self. Writing in your journal has another benefit: it helps you remember.

To get started with journaling, writing random thoughts without structure is a good way to begin. Freeform writing is without rules. Remember, no one is watching, and it is only you. Write everything that comes to mind—disregard organization. Read it back to yourself to further your thoughts. Doing this exercise will help you define your goals, dreams, and bring to the forefront your original creative work.

Look at journaling as the creation of a roadmap of your ideas that leads and gives direction to your goals, along with an insight into how to implement those ideas. The action of journaling pushes you to define your objectives, fulfill your goals, and keeps notes on hand for reference. Your journal can be a guide used to hold you accountable to yourself to achieve any goal.

Over the course of my life, I wrote in a journal that also functioned as a calendar. It was a convenient way for me to keep track of dates that marked mission accomplishment in my personal life, for military obligations, and for my other work. I also use a task management system that synchs through all my electronic devices that empowers me to create and manage my projects with ease and efficiency. It prevents me from leaving space for procrastination.

Take Breaks

Your mind and body need to rest to keep you going at your full potential. Resting is as essential as working or playing—it is not an activity to feel guilty about doing unless it is out of proportion to the other activity your life requires. Relaxing and taking breaks is a catalyst for avoiding distractions and staying on task. When you work toward your goals with clarity and in quiet with consistency, your unrested mind and body will tell you when a break is needed. Listen to your body and mind with compassion and with a greater sense of direction and balance. Take breaks and recharge your inner-self and mind; it is essential to staying productive and healthy.

If you feel you are taking too many breaks, there may be an underlying cause for the fatigue, and you must take responsibility to find a solution. Fatigue can be physical, or emotional. Be honest with yourself, ask for and be willing to receive assistance when necessary.

Meditation

Resting your mind and body is essential for staying focused. Meditation is a great method for achieving both rest and focus; it is an excellent form of controlled relaxation. If you are unfamiliar with meditation, you may misunderstand the purpose and the positive benefits associated with it. Meditation is not about getting sleepy or stopping your thought process. It teaches you to quiet your mind at your command. It can be performed anywhere and anytime as needed.

Meditation can take place when you are doing simple acts such as drawing on a notepad or closing your eyes and taking a few deep breaths. It happens when you are just sitting and listening to beautiful music. Allow yourself to be immersed in the now of relaxation and release all other pressing thoughts from your mind. Understand there will be times when meditation is needed to clear your thoughts.

The mind, just like the body, needs to breathe. Taking a short walk and even sipping from a cup of water can fuel the function of your brain. Doing these types of meditation activities inspires the pleasure center of the brain to keep working. Resting your mind will make you feel invigorated and energized.

Meditation allows you to focus, stay on task when you get back to task, and helps you accomplish more by being alert, aware, and aggressive in stopping unhealthy distractions.

A Good Night's Sleep

Getting a good night's sleep is an essential ingredient in staying focused and being more productive. Everyone is guilty of staying up later than necessary at times—by taking one last peek at social media or watching a late-night television program. While it is more acceptable to do on weekends and holidays, I think it embarrassing to be caught daydreaming or nodding off to sleep during an important meeting. I learned early on the delicate balance of getting enough sleep to function throughout the day.

The key to addressing work and the pressure of our day is to master a balance of rest and productivity. Quality sleep and relaxation are essential to real productivity, and a well-rested brain has a better command of moods and mental clarity. Being rested allows you to be hyper-focused in performing any task in front of you. Being hyper-focused leads to hitting many goals you have set for yourself.

Exhaustion leads to being unfocused, inattentive, and unable to be at peak performance. All of this will lead to task of cleaning up failures and leaving goals incomplete. Another critical negative aspect of exhaustion is that it allows your defenses to be lowered, and distractions are given easier access to preventing your forward motion.

Maintaining at least six or eight hours for your night of sleep aids in preventing illness, reducing stress, maintaining a healthy weight, and it slows the aging process. There are additional massive benefits to getting enough rest. I have seen repeatedly the strong correlation between having a quality sleep and a higher productivity rate.

Proper Eating and Exercise

Healthy eating habits that purify your body from chemicals and toxins, along with attention to breathing and moderate exercise, even massage and stretching, are all worth placing into your schedule. Setting aside time to eat well and exercise will help you to accomplish tasks and goals by renewing your energy, rejuvenating your mind for greater problem solving, and thinking.

Here are a few ways to rejuvenate and take advantage of what eating healthy, and exercise can do for you to maintain maximum health. Remember, the most precious gift you can possess is health:

- Eat your last bite several hours before sleep
- Listen to soft or meditation-frequency music
- Clear your bedroom of electronics to avoid EMF waves
- Create an environment for sleep that is natural, filled with plants and organic fabrics
- Set yourself up for morning by listing the next day's tasks before you leave the office
- Leave your work at work and make being home a place of freedom from the day's tasks
- Include exercise, or at least a brisk walk in your day
- Get adequate outdoor sunshine into your day

Be obedient to the call of natural beauty to support what you do for self-care in your life. The more natural things you can incorporate into your life, the closer you'll get to living in an enlightened state of being.

Clean Work Area

This may sound simple and almost elementary but having an excellent organizational flow within your workspace goes a long way towards allowing you to stay focused. When your work area is cluttered, it causes you to feel uncomfortable (even if you don't think it does) and can lead to distraction, anger, confusion, stress, and even anxiety. Messy stacks of paper, food packages, files, and folders can stand between you and getting things done. Having a clean work area will be one of the easiest and quickest ways to avoid distractions, staying focused, and meeting deadlines.

Some people say that they know how to live with clutter—they are comfortable with it. No judgment: comfort with physical chaos is sometimes baked into a personality. But there is a difference between clutter and filth. Know where that line is for you because the only place for filth (and things you do not need) is the garbage.

The Basics of Right-Time Management Style

As you are in the process of defining and implementing a goal, use this good advice: estimate the amount of time it will take to accomplish the goals. Look at your entire project and do a rough estimate of the duration of time you feel it will take from start to completion of the objective.

You may feel that this is difficult. At one time, so did I. My main goal when I enlisted in the military was to become an officer. Then I learned that to become an officer, I had to be a U.S. citizen, have a college degree, and some other requirements that I did not have at the time. So, to reach that goal, I had to apply total discipline, sacrifice certain things I enjoyed spending time on, and minimize leisure time in order to reach that goal. Instead of focusing on the sacrifices, my personal philosophy became this: "Whatever I accomplish in this moment, and whatever I accomplish today, are all steps to reaching my goal of becoming an officer." Then, I generated hope, put on a smile, and took the next step.

Let's say your goal is to save $1,000.00 by the end of three months. That gives you two facts to work with in terms of visualizing the goal: $1,000 and the calendar months of March, April, May. Start with where you are now, say at $0 and it's the last day of February. Look ahead and imagine yourself holding $1,000 in cash—maybe you're dressed in shorts and a t-shirt because it is May 31. Now reel yourself back to

$0 and start taking steps forward, even if your first step is to put a penny in a jar to set on your desk as a reminder that you've set a concrete goal.

The goal and task may require a long or short-term period, which could determine the achievability of the goal. Looking at the mission or goal is essential in the goal's accomplishment. Being open and honest with yourself is the first step in managing the time to make the goal happen. You can estimate your time by doing these suggested things to help you:

- Premeditation
- Realistic expectations of yourself
- Total disciplined commitment

Goals are set in your conscious mind and in your subconscious mind. Your conscious mind sets the goal and 'believes' in it. Your subconscious mind feels the goal and although it is supposed to support your conscious mind, it sometimes undermines the willpower and belief that are necessary to reaching your goal. That is why your devotion to getting the goal accomplished depends on the importance of the goal. It is in your nature to subconsciously file the goal as a priority...or... to place it on the backburner. It is up to you to know that your goal is running on two operating systems and you must keep aware of what's happening. This is why eliminating procrastination is necessary. Remember your overall goal; then focus on the small tasks that will get you there.

From my experience, tackle the most straightforward task first and then move gradually to the hardest. All this builds momentum and tells your subconscious mind that your goal is achievable.

As you take on the small steps, keep estimating your interest in the goal. When the overall goal doesn't pique your interest any longer, or you've lost the desire in your heart to achieve it, the goal will be left undone. At that point, ask yourself:

- Do I want this to happen?
- Do I care to go through this till the end?

When chasing future goals, you must apply yourself to achieve each goal to see success. If you do not, the task will not get done. The overall goal must motivate you because, over time, your interest may wane, which will leave the goal incomplete. In the beginning, assess your motivation for the project because this way you will save time and energy if it doesn't meet your expectations. It is essential to examine the big picture into what that goal will do for you in the long run. Will it help your career, your family, your finances, and your dreams? Find the motivating factor, ask yourself, and look deep to determine if the motivating factor is important enough to go the distance in accomplishing the goal.

Most significant goals do not happen overnight and take a while to complete. Some projects can take days, weeks, months, and even years. Therefore, it is imperative to understand your entire motivation toward a project. By being honest with yourself, and upon discovering the goal does not generate enough interest in you, it is best to define another goal that piques your interest. Attention and devotion will allow you to keep moving forward and doing the work necessary to accomplish the goal.

Let me add that it is best to pace yourself. Marcus Aurelius wrote, "Make haste slowly." Make a habit of pacing yourself and exercising self-control. Journal and take inventory of your progress and the actual effectiveness of your time toward accomplishing the goals. Self-examine your work and do an accurate assessment of your work progress and quality.

When you have examined your overall goal—let's go back to the example of saving $1,000 at the end of three months—and you've determined that it is necessary and do-able, it's time to break it down into steps. This is where you make a plan that takes you from start to finish in a practical way.

You may devise two plans for yourself, like the examples below, and then make a decision as to which is the best one to follow.

Plan A: Re-directing Expenses into Savings

1. Examine my annual budget.
2. Determine the best places to cut spending on something to re-direct the money into a savings plan.
3. Make a commitment to route the money from the eliminated line item of expense to a new line for collecting the money for savings.
4. Find an accountability partner to help me reach this goal.
5. Determine whether or not to continue this practice in the same way (or a different way) once the goal has been reached.

Plan B: Saving from Income Source, Short-term

1. Examine my monthly budget to determine income.

2. Work with my bank to create an automatic transfer of funds from checking to savings twice a month when cash comes in—without eliminating specific expenses.

3. Pay closer attention to my financial status over the next three months while the savings goal is in place.

4. Stop the transfer once the goal has been achieved.

5. Since this savings goal was attained, and it felt good, determine whether to continue it at a different level, or plan to do it in a new way (see Plan A).

When you start with your overall plan, you determine its viability and as you think about it, you build it into reality. Then you cross over into actual reality when you plan the steps you need to take to get there. As you can see, there is more than one way to achieve a goal and this is where you expand on your goal by being creative and make the achievement steps feel satisfying.

S.M.A.R.T. Method of Setting Your Goals

The November 1981 issue of Management Review contained a paper by George T. Doran called "There's a S.M.A.R.T. way to write management's goals and objectives." It discussed the importance of objectives and the difficulty of setting them. Here is the meaning of the acronym:

Specific: target a specific area for improvement
Measurable: quantify or at least suggest an indicator of progress
Assignable: specify who will do it
Realistic: state what results can realistically be achieved, given available resources
Time-related: specify when the result(s) can be achieved

I like, and use this method in my own life, and I encourage others to study it and see how they can best use this wise advice. Here's an example:

My first vehicle in America was a two-door 1997 Ford Probe. When I applied for a loan to buy that vehicle, the loan officer told me they couldn't guarantee the loan because of my credit history. I found that impossible and strange, considering I had never had credit before! The country I'm from didn't have this type of credit system— our only option was to pay with cash. My only option was to save as much as I could to buy the Ford Probe. So that's what I ended up doing, and I was S.M.A.R.T. about it.

S: Buying a car was my **specific goal**; building my credit was a secondary specific goal

M: My **motivation** was to buy the vehicle and save money to do so

A: The **assignment** of buying a car was necessary for my American lifestyle

R: My goal to save money for the purchase was **realistic**—and I made a good plan

T: I chose a date to complete the goal and managed money as **time-sensitive**

I ended up saving enough to buy the vehicle I wanted and began building a good credit history. A side effect of using the S.M.A.R.T. method was that I realized I could embrace performing any job that would lead to a goal to the best of my ability. I push myself to attain optimal performance within my job and every task I do. It is now in my nature. When I was serving in the military, my job was complex, and I had to be task-plus-goal oriented. It was good training.

Using the method of S.M.A.R.T goal setting, I embraced a dedicated focus to perform my job to the potential I had envisioned. I wanted and strived for optimal performance not only for myself but for my fellow workers and the people surrounding me within my job circles. I developed a personal strategic method in determining the achievability of any goal. I also developed a means of keeping track of what I needed to accomplish my goals and exploring the short- and long-term benefits of each. I want to share these with you.

Sensible Work Habits

Goals are reached by the effect of the steps you put into practice, either consciously or subconsciously. Conscious goal setting comes with the need for planning a method into your progression toward the job or task. You may have heard the question: "How do you eat an elephant?" and its answer: "One bite at a time." Approaching goals in small, achievable steps and allowing your mind to process each step are optimum smart approaches for project work.

As you lay in your steps and perform them, you'll find out what works and what doesn't.

Know that returning to a project after a short or long duration of time allows the possibility of seeing something different that you did not see before. These new ideas could enhance and lessen the difficulty of a task or process. Looking at what you could achieve by defining smaller goals can help the overall focus of the goal remain clear. Plus, focusing on smaller steps will allow you to change, if necessary, any stage to help you make the goal a reality. These small, calculated steps lead to goal success.

Approaches to Determining Goals

Determining goals and establishing the visions of each goal are vital to reaching success. You may plan on accomplishing the goal by defining the deadline as more than just a date but with a summary or list of all that had to happen to reach the conclusion. You may define every aspect of the goal and write every detail in a rough draft or list of the entire goal or project. Either way, utilizing different ways to set your goals is essential. Understanding the type of person that you are, along with knowing your style for accomplishing goals, is critical.

A problem or two may arise in how you measure goal completion. Expect this; don't get discouraged. The type of measurement system you use should match your goal.

For example, measuring for your savings goal will likely be done by money management software, or a bank. If you were to measure your savings by using an abacus, a coin purse, or some other inappropriate tool, the path to your goal may not be smooth. The key is to set up an actual method to measure the achievement of goals and make it fit with your style. You can use different techniques such as calendars, a tracking app on your computer, planners, organizers, charts, or dedicate a journal for writing about your goal and the progress you are making.

Find what works best for both the goal and you and your personality.

Some Goal Types for Success

Specific goals: Be specific in what you want to accomplish. Brainstorm to break down the goal. What is it about the goal that defines its meaning and makes you aspire to achieve it? What is the specific detail that will keep you engaged? Find the heartbeat of the goal that keeps you driving toward it by being specific. Do you want to "lose weight," or "lose 30 pounds?" Do you want to "lift weights" or "bench press 300 pounds?" Do you want to "save money" or "save $1,000 pounds... or dollars?"

Measurable goals: Keeping your goals attainable is essential in reaching any goal's potential success. As a human, you have the nature to dream big, but often, you can get caught in imagining too big and making the goal unattainable. If you cannot reach a goal within a specific time frame, that goal should be revised with a changed duration of time. Change your goal as it proceeds and follow your intuition as it develops and evolves.

The word "change" might scare you. But when you see it as freeing, healing, and unavoidable, and the more favorably you welcome it as a constant, the more positive it turns. It's best to adopt this truth and remain optimistic about its effects.

Attainable goals: Define your goals as feasible by keeping them within reach of your pace and working style. By going at your pace, reaching an achievable goal gives you a real sense of completeness. Chasing a goal outside of your style, one that is not attainable, will place your efforts on a perpetual delay. Make sure your goal is achievable by performing small steps and tackling the most manageable tasks first. This will open the details of the larger tasks ahead and prime you for the more complex and substantive material.

Here's a good example set by Joe. He wanted to lose 30 pounds, so he signed up for a gym membership. He regularly went to the gym to exercise and took time to also monitor his diet. He saw positive change bit-by-bit every day. All small steps he took got him closer to his goal—and then, when he reached it, he kept going which made him happy

Compared to Joe, Sam's goal was off the rails even as it began. His goal was to be able fly. Not as a pilot, but literally—like a bird with wings. This goal was absolutely impossible and unattainable—there is no way he'll be able to grow wings and fly like a real bird! Pursuing a goal like that not only unattainable, but also can harm him if he ever attempts to practice it. Although this is a radical example, the fun makes it easy to fit into an example.

Relevance: Is your goal relevant? Ask yourself if reaching your goal is relevant to you. Do you want to attain this goal, and will it help in your life? Will the goal uplift you toward increased finances, enhanced family life, better relationships, or business success? Examine the reasons in which you want to reach the goal. What is the primary objective, and the benefits attained once the goal is reached?

Time: length of goals to attain. Looking at the duration it will take to reach a goal is one of the key elements in meeting any successful deadline. Keeping the timeframe in the front of your mind will drive you each day to ensure you hit the mark. It is essential to plan. You can modify your schedule to adjust to unexpected things in your life. Do your best to keep modifications and extensions to a minimum. This will help you stay on track with time and with your goals.

I remember when I was getting ready for my first bodybuilding competition in 2015. My short-term goal was to be conditioned and well-defined to have a better chance to win the contest. To look conditioned and well-defined on stage, it takes time to prepare. The contest was in June, I had to start conditioning 90 days prior to the show by strictly controlling diet, training, and posing practices. I have to admit that I got tempted many times to eat a 'cheat' meal. But when I remembered the purpose of my conditioning, I resisted that temptation by reminding myself that it was temporary—just a few days—then I knew I'd be able to enjoy a large pizza with lots of cheese. So, it was a sacrifice that I had to make until I could gain the rewards: a good show at the contest, and a large, meaty, cheesy pizza!

Keep Your Goals from Spreading

I have stressed the importance of keeping your goals at the forefront of your life and pursuing them each day. Sometimes you have to assess them moment-by-moment because your conscious mind is always at play with your subconsciousness.

For example, every day when Jane wakes up, she goes through a list of short- and long-term goals before she performs them. They are: Getting to work on time, finishing a report by close of business, picking up a package at the post office, spending 45 minutes at the gym, cooking soup for dinner, and her long-term goals of saving $1,000 in three months, planning a vacation, painting the dining room, and buying a car. At certain moments in her day, she pauses to think, perhaps plan, and then prepare to take whatever small step each goal requires. Sometimes she's distracted: "Maybe I'll skip lunch to finish this report a few hours before close of business," or "It is fun using this new financial journal as I'm working out my savings plan," or, "Do I really want to paint the dining room? I'm not sure...maybe that can wait until next month," or, "I'll ask Tom to pick up that package at the post office; I don't need to do that task."

This is how Jane lives with her goals...how she carries them with her on to-do lists and how she really carries them in the imaginary suitcases of her conscious and subconscious mind.

As long as Jane keeps her goals on topic, she's on a good track. If Jane were to ditch the new financial journal, push the limits of her deadline to finish the report, or go to the and then the coffee shop and then the grocery store and then the post office (only to find it closed for the day)...her goals would have spread themselves too thin to accomplish. You probably have a better example of what happens when you plan workarounds that affect your goals.

Often, you might verbalize your goals out loud. This is dangerous territory and puts you on rocky ground. Let me explain. When an intention is verbalized, it is out in the open. In the open, others hear what you are doing, and you also listen to yourself talking about what you are doing.

When a goal is spoken about over and over, the importance of the goal begins to diminish. When this happens, it is in your nature to start seeing the goal as already being accomplished. Your goal loses steam, and you believe it is finished. When your mind adheres to the thought the goal is complete, focus on another goal steps in and takes over. This leaves the initial goal not being completed.

When you talk about your goals, you risk sabotaging your efforts. When a goal is spoken, it could be filed in your mind as something you have inadvertently accomplished.

Now, I am not saying you should keep every goal a secret. It is fine to discuss your goals with friends and family. Tread carefully when you allow the goal to become completed in your mind. Talking about your goals enables the sensation of less pressure to reach for the goal.

Keep them inside; keep them in the front of your brain. This method allows you to keep reaching to accomplish your goals. Plus, you can focus and devote every second you have to the goal.

Keep your leading goals in front of you and let nothing interfere, including yourself, in making things happen. Keep moving forward until you have hit the mark. Once you hit the mark and achieve the goal, you will see the difference in your life. Do your best to develop systems that work in your life to keep your focus; do not get lost in translation by verbalizing your overall goals and detouring your plans of finishing the goal in entirety.

Steer Clear of Perfectionism

You can connect procrastination and perfectionism in two different roles as you move toward your goals. They can be misunderstood as being almost the same, but they are different in astronomical ways. Being a perfectionist is an admirable trait and is the drive that most people use to push forward toward goals. But perfectionism can have a negative effect. Chasing after perfectionism can make you slow down and even come to a stop with your goals. When you strive to get everything perfect, the progress you are making slows down, and you allow yourself to not place the goal as high in importance.

Perfectionism can be confusing because you don't know how to make something work in the way you desire. This hinders you from reaching your goal. As a perfectionist, you get it in your head that the goal is not reachable because you can't line it up perfectly.

The fine line between perfectionism and procrastination is that to be perfect requires extra time, you feel that you cannot make the extra time, and then you slow down, and procrastinate. You put off achieving the goal because it cannot be done the exact way you imagine. Perfectionism leads to procrastination, and you must be careful to avoid both. Head off procrastination by being more flexible and open to change.

Ask yourself if you are a perfectionist. Is it in your nature that everything must be as you want it, or you stop and call it quits? Does it have to be your way or the highway? If this is you, the good news is that the act of recognizing this about yourself is the first step in making sure your perfectionism trait does not hold you back in achieving your goals.

Understanding you are not perfect, and nothing you will do will be perfect, is essential. The only perfect one is God. And you and I are not God. We are humans with faults, and no one or anything is perfect, nor ever will be. Take this idea and place it next to your focus on your goals. This idea should ease any pressure you place upon yourself. I want you to take this to heart. No one, and nothing is exactly perfect. Since none of us are absolute, the best answer is to do the very best you can with anything you do—and be proud of what you accomplished. The moment you recognize you have done the very best you can without worrying about being perfect, you will find it rewarding and easier moving forward with achieving your goal.

If you aren't careful, perfectionism can be dangerous to relationships and can alienate you from your friends and family. If you find yourself being a perfectionist, there are some questions you need to ask yourself that may help you in understanding your nature. Understanding the intricacies of perfectionism will help you to overcome the perfectionism trap, keep your motivation level high, and continue moving you towards your goals.

Sometimes, humor can soften a strict situation—a little. An example: I was raised in a culture where education was considered as the only way to achieve success. Since my father grew up in that same environment when he was child, his only focus was for his children to never stop going to school. I am convinced that if he were still alive, he would want me to have more than one doctorate degree. Back then, there was shame upon me if I was mediocre—and the standard of mediocre for my family was bringing home all A grades on our report cards. My haircut and clothing and demeanor had to be formal at all times for my parents. If I failed at any element, there was shame put on me. As the firstborn in my family, my other brothers followed everything I did, and if they did or acted in a wrong way, my dad would punish me because I set the wrong example. I was responsible for their actions—as well as my own. It seems harsh, but my brothers and I turned it into a good situation by challenging one another to achieve our goals.

When it comes to education, I guess I am almost the same as my dad was with me. I made my children believe and abide by this report card rule:

A = Awesome
B = Bad
C = Catastrophic
D = Dead (huge problem)
F = F**k no!

Do you know the difference between excellence and being perfect? Are you a perfectionist, or do you strive for excellence? Excellence and perfectionism are two different things, but to the naked eye, they seem to be the same. Both traits are similar but are on two different sides of the spectrum. They are far apart. In realistic terms, achieving excellence is not found by pursuing perfectionism.

The way I describe the pursuit of excellence is doing the right thing and focusing on the "reason" for any task to be completed, along with keeping the focus on results that are achieved.

I describe the pursuit of perfectionism as being the opposite. Perfectionism is the primary intent on doing the exact right thing but with the focus on how things "appear" along with the concern on how others view your goal and if it is completed.

Being a perfectionist can rob you of your time and drain your energy for completing a goal or task. It can beat you up inside and have damaging effects by not living up to the outcome you set to achieve. Thinking in this manner boils down to you believing that nothing you do is any good. This leaves you feeling down and kills your motivation to see things through. Perfectionism is a mirage and does not exist. Being perfect is something beyond your reach or anyone else's scope.

The answer is to train yourself to relax, do the best you can, and try not to make everything perfect. Perfection won't happen. Assure yourself by knowing you have done your best, and no one else's opinion of your accomplishment matters. Only your opinion matters.

Remember that for some people's goals, perfectionism is necessary. Think of the people who make parts for airplanes, or brakes for automobiles. Think of the parents who have a duty to protect their children from harm. These folks have to ensure that there is a level of "perfect" in the jobs they must do.

Some goals require extra time and effort for a payoff that rewards yourself and others. Then there are other goals that are less-well-defined and as long as they get done, all is well.

Here's a simple chart to consider the levels of striving in terms of short-term goals:

Perfection	Excellence	Acceptable
Driving a car	Giving a presentation	Taking out the trash
Framing a home	Cooking a meal	Dressing appropriately
Performing surgery	Passing an academic exam	Giving to charity
Paying bills	Disciplining a child	Setting a boundary

Also, what is the primary goal that is baked into the success of any endeavor? I think it is efficiency. Do you know how to strive for efficiency when making progress on a goal? Keep to the goal! Don't succumb to distractions!

For example, let me take you back to the goal of saving $1,000 in three months. As you're working towards that goal, you happen to receive some unexpected cash as a refund from a utility company. Do you use that cash to buy a new shirt, or do you use that cash to add to your accumulated savings? What is the most efficient choice? Some will say to put the unexpected money towards the savings goal. Some will say to keep on the track of saving on the plan and use the money to replace the shirt with a hole in it.

Efficiency is important when planning to meet your goals...and it is always subjective.

Chapter II
Avoid Procrastination

Have you ever just put something off because you didn't want to do it? We are all guilty in our lives of doing this. I know I have. There have been many events in my life, where I have found myself not wanting to perform the task at hand, but over the years, I pushed through and accomplished the goals. I knew I had to. In the military, tasks had to be performed as peoples' lives were at stake.

Since the dawn of man, people have suffered from procrastination.

What Is Procrastination?

A Greek poet by the name of Hesiod once spoke about this problem in his poem, "Works and Days." The entire poem is at (theoi.com/Text/HesiodWorksDays.html) and here is an important excerpt: "Do not put your work off till to-morrow and the day after; for a sluggish worker does not fill his barn, nor one who puts off his work: industry makes work go well, but a man who puts off work is always at hand-grips with ruin." Using the real poem changes the text below:

As I read that poem, the line "Do not put your work off till tomorrow" stuck with me. How does it stick with you?

Today's society mirrors this specific line. Everywhere, we find people of all ages, races, creeds, and religions, with one common denominator. Everyone is distracted by some form of major or minor distraction source. With television, radio, electronic gadgets, mobile phones, and smart watches, our environment is fixated and consumed with these multiple facets of distraction. Our minds and eyes are preoccupied with whatever is on the screen or being broadcasted. One doesn't have to travel far to witness people sitting, doing nothing, holding devices, and not moving or being productive in any manner. This is procrastination in its purest form.

Procrastination is a huge barrier that keeps you from living a full and prosperous life. At some point, in everyone's life, a person must make a choice, and the choice is simple. Choose to not procrastinate. Choose to move forward toward a specific goal.

When you choose to procrastinate, negative consequences follow.

Many adverse results are obtained when procrastination factors itself into achieving a goal. With procrastination, you could begin to feel regret and even negative feelings towards accomplishing tasks. These feelings can build, turning into more immense feelings of guilt and even shame. Procrastination leads to missed chances to prosper by squandering time, only for it to be wasted. Time is a commodity you can't get back. And when you procrastinate on a task, you are killing time along with placing yourself on a path of regret, guilt, and, most of all failure. The adverse effects of procrastination are staggering when you consider that you accomplish nothing, and your life comes to a halt. When nothing viable has happened in your life, you feel empty, and your life seems undone and incomplete.

Avoiding procrastination, not wasting time, is what allows you to invest in yourself. You accomplish what you have set before yourself, making the accomplishment an enrichment in your life and something worthwhile. One way to address avoiding procrastination is by looking at procrastination as an enemy, that shows up only to kill your time. Protect your time and face the enemy of procrastination firsthand, and soon you will reach and accomplish goals, perform better, and receive the successes that life has in store for you. When you address any task or goal, complete it as it presents itself. Perform the task at your earliest availability. Reach deep down and push yourself, avoid procrastination, and accomplish the goal (or a piece of it) that is in front of you.

Knowing and Overcoming Resistance

One of the first steps in overcoming procrastination is recognizing that it is happening. Acknowledge the fact that procrastination is what you are practicing. Knowing what you are up against when you procrastinate is crucial in developing positive habits that keep you moving.

Being lazy is not procrastination. There is a significant difference. Laziness is the development of habits formed by constantly persuading yourself not to do things. Idleness or laziness is an intentional choice to not move forward with any task or goal you have set for yourself.

Procrastination resembles laziness and can evolve into full-scale inactivity if you are not careful. I have tried in the past to take a steady path in pursuing goals.

For example, I wanted to turn my garage into a home gym. I bought all required equipment that for that project, but never made the time to put in appropriate flooring and place the equipment. Over time, this kind of procrastination cost both time and money. I had to head to the gym every day, pay for membership, and, I always got home late at night. I finally overcame the costs of such procrastination and learned a good lesson—and now I enjoy working out at home, on my own time, for free.

It became evident that choosing a relaxed direction never benefited me. By selecting these impassive directions, additional work became necessary only to achieve the same goal. I want to help you avoid this deception. It is my experience that hard work is in line with motivation and tenacity and leads to positive results. Even though it is hard to resist, choosing a laid-back path doesn't always bear the positive results we desire.

What Are the Distractions that Lead to Procrastination?

Experiencing the different levels of success in my life did not come easy. I set lofty goals and I reached them by managing, maneuvering, and avoiding distractions. The challenge was holding myself accountable by defining and identifying the major distractions that would prevent me from obtaining my goals. The initial test was avoiding the distractions once I had correctly identified them. Some distractions were challenging to overcome.

Learning the distractions in each of our lives is the initial mission that must be accomplished before any goal, small or large, can be achieved. Identifying within ourselves, examining our traits and desires is problematic because it goes against our human nature. Our inner self wants to do exciting things and provides pleasure. Distractions, in most instances, do both. We associate procrastination with tasks that do not offer fun and exhilaration.

Pure human nature points to delaying functions because we do not want to experience negative energy, thoughts, and or feelings. Distractions, at the core, are the avoidance of achievement through harmful activity and pursuing more accessible, more emotional aspects in our lives. Distractions push us off the pathways set for ourselves in achieving any goal.

The first step in identifying major distractions in my life, at the onset, was setting a goal not to allow myself to be distracted. I agreed to hold myself accountable for defining the causes of distraction surrounding my life. I understood that the act of recognizing distractions in my life would not be enough. An additional support mechanism had to be employed to be effective.

Today, there are many distractions that each of us faces. From the time we get up in the morning, distractions present themselves in different forms. Radios, televisions, computers, and mobile phones are prime examples of methods of delivering distractions. Each case is delivering a version of information aimed at gaining our attention away from the immediate task at hand. The messages are distinct distractions that direct us to perform tasks such as buying items or merely visiting a business offering the advertisement.

Understanding the purpose and recognizing these distractions is essential in examining why you procrastinate. The levels of procrastination run deep. I have discovered the simple act of thinking about procrastination can lead to the undertaking of procrastination.

The essential key to being more productive is the ability to maneuver around distractions that cause delays and interference. The method of shifting around distractions is achieved by placing the distractions front and center in your life to examine and understand which ones cause you the most delay in working toward your goals. Small distractions lead to what I refer to as "a rabbit trail" and it is where you are led astray, but then keep going further astray, like a rabbit that is hopping here and there with no goal. Problematic distractions remove you from the affirmative actions you must take toward your tasks and dissolve your time and effort in achieving goals.

From my experience in examining the distractions in my life, I compiled a list of the ones that I feel are most common for everyone in today's business climate.

Incoming Emails

Email usage among businesses and everyone across the world is vast. The service is low-cost and conducting business and performing tasks, even down to the most minute, are accomplished using email.

What are your thoughts: Is using email a distraction for you?

Email is a double-edged sword. In most occupations, email use through the office is mandatory to perform your job duties. You can consider email a distraction if you allow yourself to view unimportant emails that are not pertinent to your job. Answering emails that are not of great importance can be a significant distraction. In this situation, place your priorities and keep yourself accountable to stay focused and on task. This means evaluating email importance and being honest with yourself in which level of importance the pending emails are in accomplishing your daily tasks.

It's my guess that an average person checks email 15-20 times a day. I believe that reducing the frequency of checking email to three to five times a day evens out stress levels in your work and personal life. Checking mail is necessary for most professions, and you form habits as you welcome the adrenaline rush associated with receiving emails. Something infiltrated your mind and told you that all emails must be addressed.

I believe a reply to an email of importance must be sent right away. Many email responses can be delayed or ignored. Understand that when an email comes in, and you want to review it, you are not committing a crime. However, not every email is urgent, and not every email must be responded to immediately.

Learn to train yourself to check emails less, prioritize responses, and set a schedule to check your email that does not hinder productivity. Hold yourself accountable to check emails only during that scheduled time and stay true to the schedule. This will support you in staying on task.

Office Conversations

Offices (and home offices) are busy places filled with lots of crosstalk among co-workers or family members. If you are intentional in maneuvering around distraction, finding solace is essential even in the workplace. Inside the office environment, this could prove to be problematic. Has there ever been a time where you found an optimal place you can work alone only to discover co-workers talking near you? Talk and banter in any workspace can cause major distractions. I have been in this situation multiple times, where colleagues were talking around me, causing me not to be able to focus.

If you find yourself in this situation, excuse yourself and find another location that better suits your preference to isolate. If this occurs at your workplace, ask the person to be quiet. Isolation allows you to focus on tasks in front of you without disturbance. Noise is the contributing factor in achieving or not achieving isolation. I found one of the best methods to maneuver around noisy situations is to plug my ears with headphones or noise-canceling earbuds. And this allows me to concentrate and keep my focus on my tasks.

Social Media

In the first chapter, you read about the use of social media and the reasons it presents significant challenges when alleviating distractions. The primal urge to "know what is happening" and the human nature of curiosity by "seeing posts" is evident in social media distraction. This factor is one of the biggest challenges most of us face in our world today. Social media has grown to massive proportions and is the main pulse of our society and is here to stay.

Learning to overcome and adjusting your temperament toward social media is critical when maneuvering these types of distractions.

If blocking out a specific time doesn't seem to work, you can go to the extreme and install software that blocks your social media access on your computer or mobile device altogether. When there isn't a way to access these types of sites, the distraction is less attractive, and it becomes second nature not to want to access it. Your brain will learn that access is not available, and the desire to access it will decrease to zero. There are multiple apps and software on the market that will allow you to block any access for specific periods. Research different types of blocking software and find one that works for you.

Saying "NO"

During your day, you are faced with a multitude of decisions. You are asked by co-workers, bosses, family to work on tasks that differ from the tasks on your personal list. Responsibilities to self and others are a part of life but learning how to discern and accept assignments that won't interfere with your goals is essential. You do not need to take on all the tasks asked of you. What has been your experience in being able to say no to someone? The pressure of not saying no is significant even when you know it will add a drastic challenge to your life and work. Saying yes when you want to say no is really done in fear about letting the other person down. Your actions and responses in these situations depend on your personality. Some people do not have a problem with saying no. Others have the good nature, or the fear, to help others in need and always say yes, no matter the circumstances.

Saying yes and agreeing to do things outside of your tasks, creates additional work, and becomes a distraction from your tasks and goals. When confronted with a situation such as this, weigh your options, and be honest with yourself. Explain to the person the best way you can if you are unable to commit to doing an extracurricular task. Do your best to allow yourself to say no and explain you cannot help. This is difficult to do when you have agreed to execute most everything in the past. It will be difficult at the beginning to tell someone no and that you cannot achieve that task.

Sometimes people will take your kindness for weakness. I had a coworker to whom I always said 'yes.' For example, I stayed late after work to help him out with his project. Then he asked me the next day to help out, and I said 'yes.' The same thing happened the following two days. On the third day when I told him I couldn't help anymore because I had to take my daughter to a gymnastics class, he got mad and didn't talk to me for a couple of days.

Keep your primary goal at hand and allow yourself to stay focused by not agreeing to do everything that comes your way. Choosing your battles and staying on task removes distractions. Eliminating distractions is the primary goal, and by saying 'yes' all the time, you're creating more distractions for yourself. Learn to say no to tasks that are not beneficial to your productivity and push you toward your goal. Use your best judgment.

86,400 Seconds a Day – Equally Shared

Everyone on the planet, large or small, tall or short, infant to senior, billionaire to the homeless, has the same amount of time every day. Everyone is identical in that no one has additional time because each of us has only 24 hours each day. And in those 24 hours, there are exactly 86,400 seconds. It is incredible to think that a 24-hour period, one single day, contains that astronomical number of seconds. Even though so many seconds exist each day in our lives, they disappear quickly, showing us the vast importance of avoiding procrastination.

Yet, we all know that time never stops. The seconds relentlessly tick by, and how you use your time is your ultimate choice. The beauty in this aspect is the fact that each day your 86,400 seconds resets, allowing another opportunity to press forward with life and your goals at hand. How you spend your time and what you accomplish during the timeframe of 24 hours is based upon the decisions you make.

According to Theophastras, a Greek Philosopher who was a pupil of Aristotle, "Time is the most valuable thing a man can spend."

Every one of us wishes we had more time to achieve our goals, spend time with family and friends, and partake in more recreation, exercise, love, learning, and setting goals to accomplish more in our lives. But it's time to stop wishing for more time and living in the moment, doing the things you need and want to do while on the way to all of your goals—large and small.

Over the years, I have pursued the wrong things, and I have made my share of mistakes. We all have. There isn't any way to get around that. Making mistakes means you are doing something and learning from your failures adds value and hindsight regarding your future endeavors. Taking away something positive from every experience has allowed me to analyze my progress, evaluate mistakes, and examine the proper use of my time. This affirms that mistakes aren't failures because they reveal alternate paths that can best utilize our 86,400 seconds a day.

For example, I thought it was a big mistake to have my first child in my early 20s, but now I see it had lots of positives. We both now go the gym together in the morning, having great conversations. We don't even look like father and son; we look more like two brothers. That's a good thing!

Discovering and accepting that you have 86,400 seconds a day should motivate and inspire you to take charge. This reality should compel you to make plans and set goals with urgency knowing you share in this same amount of time each day. The harsh reality for every person is that any time wasted is time gone forever. Decide now to change your habits and view each second as the precious time you cannot get back. Your time is not stored away to use on rainy days. Be wise in how you use every second of your time; it is a precious commodity. You can't live in the past, nor can you live in the future. The reality is that you are living in the present and utilizing every second to prosper and accomplish everything in your life right now.

Time Wasters and Time Savers

Through the days I was serving in the military, time management became crucial in the operations of my team. I became adept at controlling myself and managed the use of my time to make me the most productive and organized. Looking deeper, I discovered that time management is not a new concept. I know time cannot be stopped, but it can be controlled. Through your personal decisions, your time can be utilized to produce many things of value and benefit. Time is the tool in which you measure and manage yourself.

It's important to break time management down into three categories:

Self-assessment
Accountability
Self-management

Determining what parts of your life waste time and what parts save time become apparent. It is essential to understand what areas in your lives need time management improvement. Here is a list of common time wasters:

- Mobile phones and messaging
- Interruptions by email messages
- Visitors
- Procrastination

- Undefined objectives and goals
- Desk clutter
- Need for general organization

How do you determine what things in your life are will allow you to save time? These are strategies you can employ to assist in the management of your time. Putting the following plans into practice will allow you to feel in control, focused, and positive in moving forward with daily tasks and long-term goals.

Order of Priorities: Place your work above additional tasks others have asked you to do. Getting those tasks finished for others you have committed to is important but keep your goals a top-level priority. Use this simple method of establishing priority levels in your work and tasks asked by others and yourself: establish the standards as must do, should do, and could do.

Create To-Do Lists: Defining and writing your tasks that need to be completed is an excellent way to keep your mission in front of you. Recording them in written form allows you to focus, and once the job has been completed, you get satisfaction as you mark the item off the list. There are times you will come to a standstill on any project. When this occurs, refresh your mind by resting, taking a walk, snack or drink water to clear your mind. Do what fit for you best; things that will allow you to come back fresh with new ideas in getting the task completed.

Create a Master Plan: The act of sitting down and creating a master plan will liberate your mind and open you up to seeing the bigger picture. A master plan provides a defined compass and direction to follow. Hold yourself accountable to your master plan. Your master plan can include main topics such as:

Your goals
Your dreams
Your aspirations
Your hopeful achievements
Your beliefs
Your wishes

By recognizing what timewasters are and what are time-savers is vital in understanding what pieces in our lives make us fall through the cracks. Take cautionary measures to avoid wasting time by implementing time-saving techniques. Strive for significance and do your best not to be distracted from your plan. The use of your plan is essential in meeting your goals, along with self-discipline and commitment to your master plan.

Laziness Versus Procrastination

There is an internal battle raging in all of us: the tendency to be lazy and that of procrastination. We have all fought this battle at some point. The mainstay to both laziness and procrastination is that both are a choice. We confuse these two terms as being the same, when in fact, they are opposite of each other. Laziness is the act of not carrying out any task, on purpose. We choose not to do something. This is because of not being disciplined enough in our minds to carry out the task. We can even bring laziness on by fear of not being able to accomplish a goal. It is easier to avoid a task than to see if it is impossible or possible.

Procrastination is the opposite. Procrastination is the act of putting off or labeling a task as either essential or not necessary. We evaluate a task-based upon its importance and perform the task according to its perceived usefulness. If the task ranks higher, the job, in most instances, is handled urgently. But if a task ranks lower on the scale of importance, we delay the job until another date. This is procrastination.

The qualifying difference between laziness and procrastination is that laziness tasks are graded as something not essential to do. If any task seems unattractive, it can lead to making the person not want to do the task or difficult to gather up enough energy to accomplish it. The task could be simple or complex, and laziness is the choice to avoid all tasks altogether. Acting in this manner will kill your goals and accomplish long-term adverse effects in ways you cannot see.

When going after a goal, you must remain focused and driven. Once the primary goal is set, avoid procrastination and carry out each task with enthusiasm, and push yourself in reaching that goal. Avoid being lazy and never allow the concept to make its way into your life. Habitual laziness can develop in your life before you realize it. The more you avoid performing tasks, the easier it becomes, and soon, nothing in your life will make sense or have a purpose.

Laziness can be like a disease. It is a developed pattern, complicated, and challenging to defeat. The excellent news...there is a cure. Mindset. Put your complete mind into doing every task, large or small. Focus on the result, get as much done by pushing yourself continually forward. Break free from the bounds of laziness and watch your life change. With each accomplished goal, your life becomes clear.

Examining Procrastination

Procrastination can have different attributes that most people do not recognize. One of the main ingredients of procrastination is fear. Fear of facing a large task or multiple tasks can be overwhelming and cause you to delay in getting things completed. The fear of not being able to complete a task overtakes our minds, leading us to procrastinate. This is natural because avoidance of anything that causes fear or negativity is a survival technique. It is in our human nature to put off or push away what we fear. Procrastination stems from situational discomfort, pressure, and fear.

Going back to the human nature aspect, each of us reverts to repeated behaviors throughout our lives. Throughout your life, procrastination, in some form, has been a repeated behavior pattern and can bring the perception that you are unprofessional, disorganized, and even careless with your goals and life. This isn't true. I have discovered that there are qualities associated with minimal procrastination.

Now, to be clear, I am not encouraging you to procrastinate on tasks. I only intend to bring to your attention to different aspects of procrastination that have made themselves apparent. I am exhibiting these characteristics of procrastination from my personal experience and my belief they could prove helpful through these times.

Boosts of Energy

Procrastination starts with tasks you dislike, or tasks you know are going to be tedious and difficult. When you detest a task, it causes you to slow down your energy before you ultimately get the mission accomplished. Fear of a deadline awakens your senses as the time approaches when a task needs to be completed. The adrenaline from fear is a motivator. The motivation factor is not wanting to face the consequences of an incomplete task. The fear of not hitting the mark releases adrenaline which boosts your energy, erases worry, and makes the task seem bearable. Use the adrenaline boost to get the job completed.

No Time...Work Harder and Faster

When you are crunched for time, and a deadline looms in the air, the need to get things done becomes strong. Having less time increases your desire to complete the task. Even though procrastination has taken place in finishing the task, time continues to move forward, improving your push to get the task completed faster.

One of the best ways to minimize or eliminate procrastination is to make your tasks a habit or routine. Every time you feel like procrastinating, think about the purpose of the goal you have set and the deadline for it in order to accomplish that goal.

As humans, we all procrastinate at some point, and I too am guilty of it. But, when I think about the purpose of the goal that I set before me, I immediate get on that project and start completing tasks that will lead me to the completion of that project.

Last-Minute Focus

Procrastination forces you to focus hard when you need to get a task done at the final stages of a deadline. As time gets closer to any specific deadline, your mind takes over and you become laser-focused on finishing the task. It falls back to your human instinct of basic survival. When deadlines appear, your attention becomes strong to ensure completion of the task before the time runs out.

Procrastination is a choice. The act should be handled and mastered not to be repeated in your life. High-priority projects will present themselves, and they deserve your undivided attention by planning and setting timelines to accomplish each one. Focus your mind, hold yourself accountable, define, and avoid distractions in achieving each goal set before you.

Here is an example of where I procrastinated when I shouldn't have done so. I wanted to go hiking, so I bought all required gear. When it's actually time to step out, I always find an excuse to put it off for another time. I've put it off so many times that the seasons changed and made it either too cold or too hot for hiking.

Now I'll have to wait till the season is favorable for hiking...or not. I'll have to learn how to make this choice on some perfect day for hiking and see if I want to make it a habit or part of my routine.

Chapter III
Day Management

Priority, as a principle, means to perform tasks on a first things first basis by evaluating any group of items and placing them into levels of importance and urgency. Priority levels are essential for setting yourself up to achieve your goals.

Shuffling Priorities

The act of prioritizing means that you place significance on what you want to do and not do. It is your human nature to do what you desire to do and put to the side what you don't want to do. The act of doing a less desirable task in the beginning is the correct decision for prioritizing tasks at higher levels of desirability.

For example, to stay healthy and fit, I work out every day. I make sure that going to the gym to exercise stays on my schedule because it's a very high priority for me. I hear other people say all the time they would love to exercise more but do not have the time to make it to the gym. These people give a perfect example of shuffling priorities. If something is important to you, make time for it; arrange your schedule to get that task completed. Prioritization is the practice of organizing what is essential to you and showing the importance of addressing the job straight forward by doing it. Prioritization is honoring something through the performance of the task.

Prioritization also honors yourself. Let me give you an example by asking you a question and holding up an imaginary mirror so you can see yourself answering it.

What if I told you someone on your street was giving away $1,000 every morning to anyone who went for a walk around the block? Would you make walking for that monetary prize a priority? The immense benefit of the large sum of money is the motivation that leads you to prioritize walking around your neighborhood. Your other tasks would reduce in importance in light of the money you'd gain; your other tasks would become lower-level priorities. And this would boost walking around the block and collecting the cash to the top of your prioritization list.

Honor yourself by examining your motivations to do certain tasks. Honor the tasks by knowing what kinds of payoff they offer.

Shuffling priorities occurs throughout your days and life. Referring to human nature, it is natural for you to pursue tasks that will give you the highest return for your efforts. The level of priority is equivalent to the level of the benefit. What you will receive by performing the task becomes the primary concern. Learning to test and fine-tune your preferences to overlook and accept the benefit of each, whether large or small, is essential in accomplishing all your goals. Shifting priorities can throw you off-kilter and lead to a loss of focus and failure. Take pride in every task and what you accomplish, no matter the level of benefit if it completes your goal. Through detailed prioritization, continue giving your best effort toward every task, no matter the level of importance and interest.

Generating Focus

The sensible method to accomplish any primary goal is to break down the goal into small incremental steps. Even small goals are attainable by taking one step at a time; instead of attempting to do everything at once. But, beware of seeing the breakdown like pieces of a jigsaw puzzle that have just been dumped onto the table. That's only chaos. Taking on multiple tasks, jumbled together, can lead you to not accomplishing what you have set forth to do.

The way to address any major or minor task is to examine the contents of a task and define ways to break it down into smaller increments. Look first at any immediate smaller tasks that will aid you in completing the bigger goal. You can break the goal down into manageable steps and separate the steps until the overall goal is completed. When you envision the smaller steps, the goal will seem attainable. However, looking at the goal without the smaller aspects, the goal will seem momentous and thus unattainable. Overall, this can lead to discouragement as our human nature leads us to procrastinate for fear of not being able to complete the goal. Defining the smaller steps and creating an outline of things that need to be done will help you in avoiding procrastination and discouragement.

Resting the Mind and Body

When I was in the military, as a commander, part of my duty was to provide weekend and holiday safety briefings to the troops. It was my job to give information and entertain them enough to motivate and encourage them to follow the guidelines. The purpose of these briefings was to highlight safety measures, including not to exceed two-hour driving intervals without stopping to refocus, stretch out legs and muscles, or get a refreshment. Resting every two hours during travel allows soldiers to remain energized because they could switch drivers and get to their destination in intervals. This allowed them to cover long distances and stay focused throughout the trip. It was more effective than one person staying in the vehicle behind the wheel the entire time. Long durations behind the wheel can lead to exhaustion and even a fatality.

Taking this example, you can apply it to your tasks and goals. If there is a task that is causing you difficulty, taking a break from it can energize your thoughts, body, and mind. Let me reiterate. I'm not talking about long breaks. Removing yourself to rest for a short time can help you further by coming back energized with different thoughts toward accomplishing the task. Focus wanes after long periods of study or work. Taking short interval breaks when facing challenges in your daily tasks will bring positive results and can lead to many additional assignments being completed.

Goal Setting for Day Management

In your lives, you have several goals. Large or small, you have specific goals you hope will change your lives in some manner—likely for the better. Whether it is a new job, a promotion, or to finish an ongoing project, most goals lead you in your desired direction. Each day, it presents you with possibilities, and to achieve what is possible, you must set goals. Whether long-term or short-term goals, daily task management of these goals are essential throughout your daily tasks.

Manage Your Day

During my tenure in the military, I found it imperative to manage my tasks effectively. I designed a strategic timeline of tasks using PowerPoint®. I recorded my tasks to provide a visual of what I needed to complete and the order in which to perform them. I numbered and labeled my daily tasks and placed them in front of me. It freed my mind and allowed full concentration and focus on my work without the worry of missing an assignment.

The mindset of our society today is to receive things immediately. We have become a society of what I call a "Right Now!" environment. Everything goes from zero to ten at Mach speed. Getting yourself out of the "Right Now!" mindset is the first step in moving toward your daily tasks and overall goals. The way to do that is to examine the levels of your goals and break them down into small manageable steps. Apply this process to your significant goals and daily tasks by placing your daily tasks into premeditated lists to follow throughout each day.

I spend my evenings preparing and planning the next day's tasks and listing them in order. If you are not in the habit of doing this practice, I urge you to begin.

It could present itself as difficult at the onset, but, just like anything else, the more you practice, the easier the process will become. Soon, writing your daily tasks will become second nature, and you will find an increase in your productivity while providing a more in-depth focus and concentration.

One day, I attempted to get my immediate tasks finished, but because of the additional functions, other tasks could not be completed. Having so much to do placed me further behind in getting what I needed to finish. That is when I decided to view daily tasks as a standard ruler. Once each task is done at the eighth of an inch level, you move closer to the inch mark.

Soon, you will find you have made immense progress by completing tasks, in order, without confusion or forgetfulness. The hard truth is you cannot jump from zero to ten to get what you want. There are necessary small steps in your daily and long-term tasks that must be completed. These small steps are achievements, and you should acknowledge each success and necessary to complete the task or goal in your life.

Management by Organization

My job in the military was filled with many tasks, with many different components to manage throughout my days. As the days went by, without notice, my work began to pile up around me. Stacks of papers that needed to be filed, notes, empty beverage cups, and more. I felt closed off and out of control just from the chaos of clutter around me. I took it upon myself to clean and organize my area, rearranged my desk for better workflow, and filed away all necessary documents. Once completed, my work excelled as I began to feel better, less confused because I now had a clean and organized work area.

If you work in an unorganized area that is filled with clutter, I suggest taking some time to organize or re-organize your workplace. Whether it is a home office, business office, or even your kitchen table; wherever you want to work, organize, and clean the area to make your workflow. You'll find that completing tasks becomes more natural, and the work is finished by maintaining an organized work area. Being organized will free you up to focus on the work items you are concentrating your efforts on.

How to Leave the Office on Time

One of the first things I do each day is exercise. I believe in staying healthy and being fit goes a long way toward keeping focused on my immediate and long-term goals. This was not always the situation for me. There were days where I lost track of time and worked late in the office. This led to stress, less time with my family, and made my life feel like it was out of control. I knew this wasn't good. I had to change things in my life. I attempted to organize everything in my life—from items to activities. I went about organizing my life by splitting my daily activities as was needed. Breaking them down by smallest to largest, and level of difficulty, allowed me to focus throughout the day. Completing each task helped me to leave the office and have time for my family and me.

This began by examining the obstacles I faced each day. I defined what tasks were the easiest to finish then moved to the more challenging tasks. Once I had these tasks in order, I approached each day by following this routine. I found that holding myself accountable to every job from smallest to largest allowed me to focus with more intensity on my work. Getting these things done kept me focused and from being distracted or tired. By reaching and finishing my tasks each day, I could get myself out of the office on time and could go home and enjoy my family. This helped me and my family become closer and stronger as things became apparent that I'd made it a priority to be home on time. My family needed that in their lives.

Define every task in your life from largest to smallest. Organize those tasks and balance your day by examining what is necessary for you to accomplish. Do the tasks that take care of you, whether its exercise or meditation or even reading a book to start your day. Observe whatever that task is for you and follow that path. Then pursue the rest of the tasks to balance your life. Do your best each day to hold yourself accountable for doing the tasks in order, reaching for clarity and balance to ensure you don't work extra. Your life can feel chaotic if working late becomes a habit. Not being home on time hurts you, your health, and your family. Prepare lists of your tasks for the following day. Follow the list each day and hold yourself accountable to those tasks to get things finished on time. You will discover you will have more control over your life and time.

Declining Extra Tasks of Others

In the early days in my military career, I worked hard to accomplish everything that was asked of me. My superior officers requested tasks for me to complete, and I strived to achieve each one proficiently and on schedule. I soon was the go-to person for most of the functions within our company. At first, I could hit the marks, but soon, I found the increasing workload was placing me behind on my tasks. I examined the situation, and I realized that people mistake kindness for weakness.

They handed me extra assignments because I never turned them away. I placed immense responsibility on myself by saying 'yes' all the time.

Learning to say no to someone is sometimes challenging. The act goes against your human instincts. It is in your human nature to want to help others but examining your workload and understanding your work method and style, it is acceptable to say no. I know that human nature pushes you to please others, to help them with their projects. It is difficult to turn someone away when they ask for help with a project. The good news is it can be done politely and respectfully.

When asked to perform a task you foresee causing you to fall behind on your current task say, "I'm sorry, I'm busy right now. Give me a few minutes to complete this task and then I can help you." Always be polite when you say no. You do not want to hurt anyone's feelings. There will be times your response might offend others. Expect that situation to occur if you have a habit of saying yes to everything coming your way. Saying no will be a shock, and they will not know how to react. In most instances, when a person doesn't understand how to respond, they revert to showing anger. Calm them down and lift them back up by explaining why you have to say no and stand firm on your decision. Do your best to get your immediate work completed, and only then, if you can take on an extra work task, allow yourself to do it. But do it on your terms. If you cannot complete the task, be respectful to yourself and the other person and say no.

Take Control of Your Inbox

Each day, you face many tasks. Email is an essential tool for most everyone. You conduct business through email, leads are generated, and products are sold throughout the email medium. These electronic letters can cause distractions and delays in your work. Taking control of your email usage is vital in staying focused and keeping up your productivity.

I have researched many methods to take control of my email usage. I used to check it all the time and found task accomplishment was falling behind. Then I discovered a system called the Eisenhower Box. Long before email, president Dwight Eisenhower created methods to control his productivity that still work.

President Eisenhower, the 34th President of the United State, served two terms between 1953-1961. Eisenhower was a five-star General in the United States Army. He also worked as the Supreme Commander of Allied Forces in Europe during World War II. Eisenhower used his productivity methods to execute invasions of North Africa, France, and Germany. He had an innate ability to maintain and increase productivity. He would maintain high levels of productivity for years and even decades.

Eisenhower's Box, a method to increase personal productivity, was developed as a straightforward, simple decision-making tool that you can learn and use for handling email. Eisenhower's Box can help you in separating your email decisions and actions based upon four fundamental principles:

- Important and urgent (complete immediately)
- Important, but not urgent (schedule to do later)
- Urgent, but not important (delegate to others)
- Neither urgent nor important (eliminate)

You can apply these four main principles to any task or goal, whether long-term or daily tasks. Apply these principles to your email inbox and hold yourself accountable by asking yourself questions based on these four principles. Set a definitive schedule to check your emails. Find the time that works best for you, either the first thing before you start your day or in intervals throughout the day. The goal is not to break your productivity by continuous checking of your emails.

One of the essential methods to avoid email distraction and taking control of your inbox is the proper setting of notifications. If you have your notifications set to alert you on your desktop every time an email comes in, it causes you to lose focus. My advice is to turn off email notifications for specific periods, preferably during work hours, to maximize your work and productivity.

Small Steps and Their Power

Performing larger tasks is best handled by breaking the steps down into smaller, more doable steps to achieve your overall goal. Often, by looking further at an enormous task or goal, intimidation can overwhelm, and avoidance of the task occurs. The urge to avoid a sizeable perceivable task is immense and can lead to neglecting or abandoning the task. To prevent this, you need to learn to define goals by dividing the goal into smaller tasks. Performing the smaller task leads to accomplishing the goal efficiently with less difficulty. The problem is that broad goals are psychological and can be perceived as more complicated than the actual task. Examining the purpose in smaller steps frees your mind to understand the goal is achievable by undertaking one step at a time. It's daunting to view a goal as one enormous challenging task that needs to be completed.

43

After you are born, there are things you learn in stages: to crawl, climb, walk, and run. The power behind those small steps is intense, considering it takes patience, effort, and performance of the smaller stages to reach the goal. Babies learn to get off their stomachs, to their knees, to being upright, walking, and running. Accepting each task and breaking each one into small steps and working on those steps until you are ready to move to the next step is essential in achieving challenging long-term goals. You can even break daily tasks down in this manner to accomplish them and still maintain high levels of productivity. The power in productivity is performing functions in smaller incremental steps in pursuit of each goal or mission presented before you.

Chapter IV
Let it Become a Habit

Knowing yourself and who you are is essential in avoiding procrastination and in building substantial work and life habits. Examining yourself and finding your true potential are the first two steps in positive habit-forming.

Unblocking Yourself by Knowing Yourself

I have discovered over the years that there is a fine line between self-confidence and arrogance. I have witnessed many people cross the line and come across as arrogant. Even though they were trained in their skill set, the arrogance they displayed made it an unpleasant experience to be around them. Understanding who you are as a person, focusing on your skills, and being kind and humble will help you avoid the mistake of confusing arrogance with being self-confident.

As a former military officer, I have built active skill sets and developed habits by learning who I am and by presenting myself constructively. I know I am self-confident in my life and the work that I provide. However, I understand who I am. I am a calm and humble person who has skills and high qualifications in my field, and I present my skills in a modest and self-confident manner. I make sure that my actions do not display arrogance. I value and represent my strengths and skills by avoiding arrogance.

Recognizing who you are and having the confidence to display your strength and value is essential in forming healthy habits. Understanding your value and self-worth is also necessary. Revealing what you are capable of will place you on a positive path to unlock your potential. The value of a person shows through the performance; along with their expertise. Do not be afraid to talk about your skills, who you are and what you can do; only do it in a manner that avoids arrogance.

For example, when I was in the military, many of my co-workers would ask me for help in accomplishing their tasks. I would help them because I had the skill sets and knowledge to help them complete their daily work. Everyone came to understand I knew what I was doing, and I never had to proclaim it or display arrogance. I portrayed my skills by performance and not in an unhealthy manner.

Believe in yourself and the skills you possess. Look at your skills as a valuable tool. Developing good habits starts by examining yourself and recognizing your skillset as unique and essential. Understanding who you are will aid in breaking bad habits and moving you forward in your work and life. Know the person you have become, and most of all portray humbleness, kindness, and professionalism to those around you.

Reprogramming Methods for Forming New Habits

Implementing an improved mindset and reprogramming your negative habits into productive habits is essential in your life. Everyone has to do daily tasks that are repetitively performed sub-consciously; for example, placing your car keys in a certain spot so you will always know where they are located. This simple act of repeating positive habits saves you time from looking for your keys around your home. Re-learning your habits falls into the arena of time management and goal achievement. Many aspects of your life can be repeated diligently to save time and help you become more productive throughout your day.

Training yourself to repeat positive actions that move your progress forward in your daily and life goals is essential to achieve. Over the long-term, taking charge of your negative habits and applying dominance toward your positive actions saves time and energy. Look at the tasks you do daily and ask yourself the following questions:

Is there any aspect of my life I could improve?

How can I do things differently to achieve better results?

How can I apply these new habits to my life?

What are the bad habits that hurt my productivity and life?

Examine your everyday jobs from the smallest to the largest, most challenging responsibilities that come up for you every day. What can you do to make those tasks easier? Taking charge of the way you do things, and repeating positive tasks, develops many strong habits that help you in your daily life. Approaching your habits with a positive mindset and intent to make things work better will help you develop good habits across many areas of your life.

Smart Work Habits for Long Term Success

Having positive work habits, over time, places you on the path to long term success. You can apply smart habits to other significant areas of your life. You can implement positive habits in your personal life with family, children, side businesses, and hobbies. And you can take the experiences found in your work life and apply the same principles to your non-working life to achieve better relationships, more income, more joy, and a better life overall. If you discover habits that are helpful and positive in your work career, then there isn't any reason not to use these habits in your daily life to help you move toward success in your entire life.

Do your best to have healthy positive habits, along with developing a routine of implementing them into your life. You will see results by practicing good habits, which will lead you to efficiently getting things accomplished. For example, taking scheduled breaks is one positive habit that will increase productivity and keep your energy level higher. If you work too long without resting your mind, you will feel sluggish and exhausted, which leads to incomplete work and production goals not being achieved.

I have studied different countries that promote taking breaks and resting your mind. Many countries believe in relaxing and taking breaks to reinforce higher productivity. In Spain, the lunch break time is between 2 pm and 5 pm. This explains the seriousness of the word "siesta." In Spain, most companies make it mandatory to break between those hours due to the heat of the day being at its highest. Studies found throughout companies in Spain, whether the employee works inside or outside, their attention span and productivity take a nosedive because of the excessive heat.

In France, companies and the French people alike have discovered that shutting down between 2 pm and 4 pm has led to less stress, more productivity among workers and school children universally. The leaders of France embraced the use of taking an extended break to re-energize, decrease stress, and increase productivity. The entire country, at the specific time, shut down their shops, schools, companies, and businesses across the country to take a two-hour lunch and rest. These types of habits of resting, taking breaks, planning, and implementing positive habits have shown to increase production, and attention spans in the workplace and our lives.

Break Old Habits and Bring in New Habits

Daily habits help you in everything you do—everything from brushing teeth to enjoying a cup of coffee in the mornings. You rely on your habits to maintain regularity in your daily life. Formed habits push you along and get you through your days. There are good habits that produce positive outcomes, and there are bad habits that provide adverse results. Habits are either wrong or right for your goals and life.

By recognizing your habits as human behaviors that are either useful or detrimental you have the power of shaping and categorizing the specific habits in your life. When examining goals, productivity, and time management, negative habits need to be tamed, broken, or changed to reflect positive habits and productivity.

There are many tools available to help you form and break habits that have a negative influence over your life. Digital books, electronic gadgets, and software applications, designed to help you pinpoint a pattern or to change it, are available. The only downfall is these different mediums, in most instances, are designed with the idea that it takes 21 days to make, or break, a habit. This 21-day theory is based upon findings of Maxwell Maltz, M.D., a plastic surgeon in the 1960s who claimed in his book *Psycho-Cybernetics* that on average it takes 21 days for any of his patients to get accustomed to their new faces and features.

The time needed to change a habit is unknown. I have discovered that it takes an average of 66-70 days for a new habit to be formed or changed. The reason is that everyone is different, and the patterns formed by different individuals, either negative or positive, are different in complexity and importance. Developing a new practice takes time, and breaking bad habits takes additional time and effort. Don't expect to break bad habits overnight or in a few weeks. Over time, if you make yourself start a routine of breaking bad habits with a serious mindset, your life will see improvement in many areas. Breaking a negative habit is synonymous with creating and establishing new positive habits. Replacing a bad habit with a good habit is the start of building a productive life. The only catch is breaking habits isn't done in a specific duration of time. You cannot predict it.

Because there have been no studies done (that I'm aware of) regarding the amount of time it can take to break a bad habit, I suggest that you set a time for yourself, and use a formula that is specific.

When you have a habit that is not serving you, look at how long it took to build it up, how long you've been doing it, and how much you want to stop. Each habit will be unique unto itself. For example, if you've been smoking a pack cigarettes per day since your teen years, you're now 50 years old, and you have several good reasons to quit, then estimate the amount of time you'll need until you can celebrate the ending of the habit. This type of habit may require medical supervision, the assistance of drug therapy, and the building in of counteractive habits (such as eating a carrot stick when the urge to smoke arises). For this person, it may take six months before the need to inhale tobacco smoke has become a thing of the past.

As you make a commitment to stop destructive habits, the only certainty is that you must face the habits, be secure about releasing them, and be diligent about making changes to keep the habit from making a comeback. Be open and honest with yourself about specific practices that are not productive and positive towards your goals. For extra assistance in your efforts to eliminate a bad habit, find an accountability partner, hire a life coach, keep a chart, plan to journal your progress, or find some other method or modality (perhaps hypnosis) that works for your situation.

Old Habits...Not So Bad

Old habits should not always be considered bad habits. Your old habit of watching TV before bedtime is not so bad—but it could be better if you decided to read for 30 minutes before sleep. Old patterns could be habits that are non-effective or productive in your life any longer. Observing our old habits and whether they are effective is something you need to decide. Changing how you function by altering your habits, removing any bad habits, and replacing them with good productive habits is a great step toward pursuing your goals.

If you look hard enough, in most instances, you can find old habits that do not add benefit to your life. Doing them may not be wrong, just not practical. Use your motivations, your specific circumstances, and your personality to change the old habits you have discovered as unproductive in your life.

Willpower

Willpower is the control you exert to do something or to restrain yourself from an impulse to do something. You've formed most of your negative habits by not having enough willpower—and you've added the energy of procrastination to keep you from making changes that will be better for you. When you have control over something in your life, along with the frame of mind to monitor and maintain the time to perform the task, you can say that you have willpower. Managing your willpower to take control and break bad habits or establish control over something that you want to do is right. This involves the responsibility you owe to yourself. You must be able to control what you're doing, and the times you do it, for willpower to be effective. Only you can give yourself the power to recognize this and make it a powerful truth in your life.

Asserting yourself to get work accomplished takes endurance and willpower. People put off or delay doing what they don't understand. Learning about something takes additional effort, and if you do not know how to do something or fear making a mistake, it will lead you to delay the task, or not do it at all. Willpower must take precedence over your desire to push yourself to get things accomplished. Throughout your daily life, you need to use your willpower to push yourself to complete work that is less desirable. You have to get those tasks out of the way in order to reach your goals. Using willpower to establish positive habits and to break old/bad habits is essential in creating a sustainable, habit-formed, and productive life.

Chapter V
The Power of Productivity

Every person at one time or another has felt inadequate and has lacked self-confidence. Being self-confident parallels feelings of self-esteem. Self-esteem plays a significant role in everyone's life and having a healthy sense of self-esteem directs your decisions and your life in the right ways.

Enhancing Self-Confidence with Time Management

Everything begins with healthy self-esteem, which leads to being self-confident, which provides the courage to face challenges in front of you in your life. Enhancement of self-esteem is something you must do for yourself—find what emotional blocks you have and work on healing them. Enhancement of your self-confidence can be done through proper time management.

Having your time management systems in place is essential; it is an indispensable aspect of your short-and long-term goals. Lack of time management, when it mixes with lack of self-confidence and self-esteem is a recipe for failure. The direct effects of a lack of time management leads to stress, fatigue, and depression.

To avoid these scenarios and keep you on track, I have developed specific formulas that you can use to cultivate a successful time management strategy. Apply these formulas to your daily, weekly, and long-term goals:

- Delegate
- Plan each day
- Use a schedule
- Make exercise a habit
- Consume proper foods

Delegate

There are many tasks that need to be completed daily in order to accomplish small goals. Sometimes in your work life, you will reach a point when the workload is more than you can handle. When your workload becomes heavier, trying to do everything yourself can work against you causing stress, anxiety, and feelings of being out of control. When this occurs, delegate the small tasks to someone else. If you are not in a position of leadership, ask colleagues to lend a hand and return the favor when asked. Significant problems arise when your tasks increase, and your time decreases. When this occurs, and you see yourself getting less done, delegate work, and do not perform everything yourself.

There is a small amount of pride attached to trying to handle your work by yourself. You can look at this positively. Don't be afraid to ask someone to help you with your workload. There is French saying: Qui ne risque rien, n 'a rien, and it means, "He who risks nothing gains nothing." So, don't be intimidated by fear—ask for help. By asking someone to help you, you are providing an opportunity for that person to learn about the job and become better at what they do. Delegating work may also inspire the other person or instill encouragement by entrusting them to do the job. These are positive aspects of releasing pride and assigning work to others to help you manage your task and time. Help others by assigning them tasks and let them know they are training and learning skills to help them along in their position and career. Understand that by delegating, you are helping others to learn.

Home life lends itself to delegation. At home, all members of the household should contribute to tasks that need to be done to have a harmonious living space. Some families or groups of roommates have a natural leader in their group—this person keeps everyone else on task. Some groups work as a committee to assess and delegate tasks.

Both at work and at home, delegation is something that requires negotiation, good exchange, and cooperation. Do all you can to be effective at it. If necessary, remind all the others in your life that each of you has the same number of seconds in a day and they should be used well for the good of all individuals in a community.

Plan Each Day

Planning is something I enjoy—and you can learn to enjoy it, too. Every day, I take time after the workday to plan my tasks for the following day. This time management task is the piece of the puzzle you must do daily to be successful with your goals. The effect on my life by planning each day with specific tasks and marking them off once completed is liberating. All of this leads to improved health, less stress and confusion in my life. Take time out for yourself and write out your tasks for the following day. Place them in your calendar or make notes on a notepad. Whichever method you are most comfortable with, make this habit a consistent practice. You will have a sense of accomplishment and satisfaction when you complete every task. I cannot go a day without doing this—even weekends. I plan what I will do with my family and do my best to follow the tasks and get them done.

You will need to discipline yourself to put this step into practice. Once you make it happen, you will see maximum results within your work and personal life.

Planning your day guides and helps you in many ways. Planning your tasks for daily, weekly, and yearly goals will keep you accountable and on track. Discipline yourself to follow the plan and do your best to not deviate from the program you set. When situations arise that are out of your control, referencing your daily plan can provide answers to determine if the extra actions required of you can be done or if you need to delay or delegate the responsibility. Obviously, in emergency situations, you have to go with the flow of the situation, show up for it, or for the person involved, and then take some time after the crisis to re-orient yourself to the life you want to live in the way you want to live it.

Use a Schedule

Once you have an overall plan for your day, set aside time to schedule your day all the way down to the fun tasks. Adhere to your schedule the best way you can. By managing your schedule, you will be more productive. Sticking to your schedule will show you where the distractions are in your life. It will take some effort and diligence to develop steady habits to stay on track with your schedule but doing so will be worth the effort. Your productivity will reach higher levels as you adhere to your schedule. Remove all distractions and use your best judgment on the calls and messages that come in as distractions. Evaluate the importance of each task, and if things arise that need to be addressed, take care of them and then proceed back to your schedule.

Make Exercise a Habit

Most of us have jobs where we sit behind a desk in front of a computer. This sedentary lifestyle for eight hours in a day can have adverse effects on your goals and time management. Staying healthy through exercise should be an essential part of your day. Place exercise into your plan and onto your schedule each day. Treating your body right, eating healthy, and building and maintaining muscle is right for your mind, strength, and endurance.

Exercise is an essential part of my days. On average, I spend one hour and 15 minutes at the gym, Monday through Saturday. I have dedicated this time to working out, which has helped me be more productive, stay physically healthy, and has increased what I'm able to produce. I understand it may not be the case for everyone so just do the best you can. I've also been involved in many sports activities since I was 6 years old. This long-term dedication to sports and physical activity has become an essential aspect of my life. It has grown to become a lifestyle for me.

During my tenure in the military, I made sure that everyone in my company had at least a minimum physical appearance of fitness that was required to meet the standard for mission accomplishments. My dedication to physical health and the health of my men saved my life and many others.

Consume Proper Foods

Eating healthy is the first step to staying productive and achieving your goals. Everything you do depends on keeping yourself healthy. The Greek philosopher Hippocrates said, "Let food be thy medicine, and let medicine be thy food." Hippocrates recognized the importance of food as fuel for the body. Other authors have written thousands of books and articles on the benefits of eating healthy. You know yourself that good overall health begins with the food you ingest.

On your journey toward productivity and reaching your goals, do your best to eat a healthy diet. Eating healthy is also good for your mood, reduces stress, strengthens your mind, improves memory, and prevents strokes and heart disease.

Another excellent benefit of eating healthy is looking and feeling better about yourself. When you feel better about yourself, you gain more confidence, making your production increase. This allows you to reach levels of productivity that will surprise you.

Productivity and Overarching Goals

Throughout your life, there have been obstacles and goals set before you. One crucial aspect of any future goal, whether large or small, is to examine how the goal could impact your life. In what ways will the goal lead you to where you want to be in your life? This process begins with breaking down the goal into small sectors to help assess the purpose and determine how it can be achieved. Here are some things to consider about vision and the overarching goal.

Vision: The vision of the goal is what you hope to achieve at its completion. The vision statement would be what you hope to accomplish along the way ending with a positive result.

Mission: The mission is the section of the goal where you list the smaller fragments that make up the entire goal. Your mission items must be in line with the vision you have set for the goal. For example, you could use the following suggestions on this list:

• Identify priorities

- Assess productivity
- Do research
- Evaluate
- Collect data

Overarching Goal: The overarching goal is everything there is to know about the goal. This is about your interpretation and creativity as you shape specific goals. Here are a few words to use as you design the complete picture of your goal:

- Attain
- Achieve
- Create
- Promote
- Stages
- Results

Being productive is the reason, force, and motivation to accomplish every goal, large or small. Increasing your work ethic, improving your attitude, and strict management of your time factor in together to help you reach your overarching goal. Striving for significant goals takes persistence, courage, and creativity. When you set a broad, overarching goal, the way to achieve it is by listing and performing the small tasks that lead to the result.

You can use this method in your everyday tasks—you can practice it with a plan to clean out your garage, create a garden, pay off debts. Develop a specific strategy that works for you to make your goals a reality. Eliminate any obstacles or issues and remain focused on each goal by using your skills and tools to reach your goal.

Everyone is different, and each of us has special abilities unique to us. I invite you to visit (pkpoteau.com) where there is plenty of information regarding goal setting, habits, procrastination, and lifestyle improvements. To reach any significant goal, it will take planning and unique skills to get there. Learn to divide the goal at hand, utilize your skills, and eliminate major and minor concerns to reach your goals.

Follow Through on Challenges

When I was in the military, someone told me I couldn't be a drill sergeant or an officer because of my speech accent. I used these impertinent comments as seeds to further my education and maintain an exemplary discipline record to reach my goals. I never let my native, accented, unique way of speaking stop me from moving forward. I faced the challenges and proved to myself by going on to attend school to become a drill sergeant and I even graduated with honors. Next, I obtained my undergraduate degree with distinction, earned two master's degrees, a project management certification, and a doctorate degree. I never lost my accent, and, I enjoy telling people about my origin in Haiti.

Throughout my life, I have met several naysayers. These are people who, for one reason or another, felt the need to push their opinion on me, to tell me of what I could or could not accomplish. Everyone has encountered naysayers. My advice is to listen to them—they'll give you a challenge. The key is not to believe them! Follow your internal voice. That voice is your spirit guiding you to reach the goals you've set forth and your dreams of accomplishing them. This is always the right course of action.

Listening to naysayers harms your self-esteem when you believe what they say and let them have power to stop you in your tracks. Do not let this happen.

Everyone endures challenges in their life. Many thought I could not accomplish the things I've done because of the way I spoke. What they did not recognize is that no matter how I spoke, I was understood on many levels. People realized my skills by watching my actions, and then listened to what I had to say. Under my command and authority, even after being in multiple gun battles, the troops comprehended and respected my command. Everyone realized my main concern and number one priority was making sure everyone survived. In those dire situations, my accent was not a deterrent, and it did not stand in the way of my command and duties. All 35 men under my leadership returned home to live with their families.

Resistance Syndrome

Resistance syndrome is what every person has the potential to do to prevent accomplishing a goal. We are all guilty of promises made to ourselves to improve our lives and achieve our goals. I have done it; I am guilty of it. Each of us, at some point, has fallen under resistance syndrome. Telling yourself, "I will lose weight," or "I will go to the gym," are promises that get resisted! These types of promises are internal. They are often broken because of poor time management, lack of willpower, mis- understanding, low self-esteem, forgetfulness. These are all examples of Resistance Syndrome.

Why do you resist? How can you make resistance work for you instead of against you?

You have a responsibility to yourself to face daily challenges, along with addressing long-term challenges and goals. Responsibility is affected by Resistance Syndrome.

Avoiding personal responsibility—not being accountable to yourself—reduces changes you want to make to your life. Resistance Syndrome keeps you stuck, making it challenging to move forward. To avoid this scenario, you need to be progressive and aggressive in meeting your challenges. With hard work and diligence, and by escaping resistance, problems will soon become defeated.

What do you do to recognize when you are not getting something done? Here is an acronym: RESIST. It stands for Recognize, Energize, Synchronize, Itemize, Standardize, Theorize. Let's break it down to be useful:

Recognize. Face your lack of desire to take action.

Energize. Generate positivity by finding small things to do that will carry you forward, let you chip away at the goal.

Synchronize. Pick up the pieces of the puzzle and as you put them together, let yourself see how all that you do is meant to happen in the time it takes to happen.

Itemize. Once you've made some headway, make a list of what you've done and what still must be done. See where you still have resistance and work on overcoming it.

Standardize. Use tools like planning and scheduling to keep you on the 'move forward' track (as opposed to the 'stand still' track).

Theorize. Look at all you're doing or have done to accomplish this goal. See that you created a theory that is unique to it. Name it: Bob's Theory of Buying a New Car, or Sally's Theory of Happy Children Doing Chores.

Once you learn to exert willpower over yourself, challenges become less bothersome and increase strong self-perseverance and independence. The way to accomplish this is to put yourself first and implement stringent rules on yourself; and do your best to alleviate self-criticism. This form of criticism can transform into fear. Fear is a primary symptom of resistance and can stand in the way of achieving your goals and dreams. Do not let yourself be intimidated by fear. Once you face your fears, in most instances, you discover that fear was more significant in your mind than in reality.

An example from my personal experience is about being afraid to speak a foreign language because I thought people would ignore me because I'd make mistakes or be misunderstood due to my accent. What I found when I allowed myself to speak in my non-native language was that people paid more attention to me—not less. In a situation like that, it's all about knowing what you're talking about and being patient with those who are working to understand what you're saying.

Successful people who achieve many goals do their best by alleviating concerns so they can conquer their goals.

Achieving Consistency

You must maintain consistent, positive habits to complete your long- and short-term goals. Managing your goals depends on being consistent in repeatable actions to reach the completion of the goals. Daily tasks that lead you to move your life forward. Conscious tasks, like brushing teeth, through daily repetition move into your subconscious. The overall goal is to complete the day with repetitive positive tasks to reach your specific goal

Throughout my life, I have witnessed a disconnect between the ways people manifest their dreams. From my perspective, it seems like some people disengage from the importance of being consistent. Being consistent goes together with being persistent toward your everyday and long-term goals. Developing and building upon your passion and drive will involve the constant pursuit of your dreams and goals.

What happens when a goal seems unable to be accomplishable? When a goal cannot be managed, it should be reset by using the S.M.A.R.T. method.

All your thoughts, whether positive or negative, within the 86,400 seconds in each day, must be filtered, and repeated continuously. Your ideas must be filtered to move from your conscious to your subconscious and vice-versa. Being consistent with negative patterns has adverse effects and brings negative results on every aspect of your life. All of this can place significant obstacles in front of you in achieving your goals.

How Do You Measure Results for Self-Assessment?

Every goal you set, at some point, must be evaluated to see where you are in achieving the goal. Even after a goal is complete, it is good to assess the steps taken to reach that goal. You should measure these steps for time, difficulty, and repeatability. Self-evaluation allows you to discover tasks you can use to achieve your next goal to save time and improve predictability. It is good practice to measure the progress of each goal, especially your long-term goals, to ensure you are staying on track. Life, in its busyness, has a way of taking us off course and into uncharted waters.

Self-assessment allows you to examine where you are within reaching your goals, and if you are not where you need to be. Then you need to reassess yourself with a change of habit, attitude, and tasks to complete to get back on track.

Self-Assessment Checklist

The benefits of self-assessment foster goal achievements for a lifetime. When you build self-evaluation into each day, it allows you to discover flaws and opportunities to correct mistakes. Creating your internal checklist and external self-assessment checklist to represent your progress is essential for staying on track with your goals.

I encourage you to begin a daily, monthly, quarterly and yearly assessment of your progress toward your goals. Being honest and holding yourself accountable is the key to using this method. Set your goals according to priority and level of importance then base your checklist on the importance of goals you have set. The self-assessment opportunities you structure for yourself should point toward how well you are doing and what you are accomplishing to reach your goals.

Use your checklist to heighten the awareness of your principles and values toward achieving your goals. The keys to a successful self-evaluation are being forthright and honest in your approach, and frank with yourself. Evaluate adverse outcomes as being as important as positive outcomes. Create your specific list of questions that will help you write an honest self -assessment. Here are a few suggestions to get you started:

- Things I often do toward my goals...
- Things I occasionally do toward my goals...
- Things I never do toward my goals...

It's Difficult to Self-Assess

I understand the difficulty of examining yourself for flaws or negative aspects. Allow another trusted individual, who will deliver an honest assessment of you, to provide you feedback on your goals, and the progress the observer sees you making. Having a fresh set of eyes, along with a different perspective, helps you stay on track through the stringent evaluation and observation you are also doing for yourself. Ask for feedback and hold yourself accountable for the assessment. Set it up with your observer to receive constructive criticism so you can take the feedback as positive and not a negative, mean reflection of you. Use the feedback to improve yourself, following in the spirit of accomplishing your life's goals.

Chapter VI
Enjoying Life

My goal throughout the book has been to encourage you to examine your entire life and help you manage your time efficiently.

Benefits of Time Management

Time management expands into your life as you strive to achieve all your goals. Managing your time is a skill that affects everything you do. There are major benefits it provides and how it has a positive influence on your life.

Reduce Stress

Managing time allows you to be in full control of what you do every day. When you know what is expected of you and what tasks you need to accomplish, it reduces anxiety and stress. When you do not manage time, things get out of sorts and cause panic and stress to happen; which is not suitable for you in any manner.

Without time management, hours and days pass without anything being finished, and not having things completed makes you feel overwhelmed; it creates high levels of harmful stress. Stress can hurt your productivity and even have adverse effects on your health and relationships.

Stay Focused

Time management is a way to stay focused on the things you must do. Stringently managing your time forces you to stay focused and get your tasks completed on time. To keep on task, you need to understand what motivates you and find your purpose. The jobs you have must interest you and serve a mission to help you stay focused, or the project will wane.

As I a young man, I wanted to compete in weightlifting and bodybuilding. I dreamed of competing and stepping on stage to show what I had accomplished. I placed posters on my wall of famous bodybuilders for motivation to keep me going, and they kept me focused on the purpose. I would wake up every morning to go to the gym, and I looked at the posters for inspiration.

When I set out to write this book, I knew I wanted to help others achieve goals through time management. It was a desire and a purpose I believed in. I stayed on task, managed my time, and completed the goal. Find what motivates you and keep the target in front of you. Allow time management to drive you to your goal by easing stress and keeping you focused.

Stop Procrastination

Time management is essential in avoiding procrastination. Delaying and pushing things off for another day leads to failure and tasks not being completed. Managing time holds you accountable for getting things done and reduces procrastination in your life. Procrastination is the biggest culprit of stealing time and wasting it. Putting things off causes stress, and stress can cause problems in your workplace, work and personal relationships, and affects your family and your own life. Do your best to avoid procrastination by managing your time and keeping yourself motivated with a purpose.

Increase Self-Confidence

One of the best benefits of proper time management is that it increases your self-confidence. Accomplishing goals through stringent time management also helps your self-esteem. You feel good about yourself and discover inner strengths. You've likely felt good feelings of accomplishment when a significant task reached completion. Time management increases your overall self-confidence by getting things done, and it helps in recognizing your self-value. When you discover what you can do and understand how you can accomplish many things through managing your time, it feels good inside.

Increase Productivity

Managing your time efficiently leads to increased productivity. You work toward small and large goals daily. When working toward your goals, time management is the main measurement of your productivity. Beware of spreading yourself too thin by helping others; you'll lose your own productivity. Although helping others is a good thing, it can get out of control and lead you to decreased production in your work.

Keep in mind it's fine to say no to someone when you need or want to stay on track with your tasks. You cannot please everyone. The best thing you can do is be polite, but don't take on extra assignments from others unless you are sure it won't affect your production. Staying on task keeps you focused, alert, and aware of what needs to be done, the closer you get to finishing the task. Completing your work improves your self-confidence along the way.

You will get more things accomplished by managing your time and being aware of any delays or procrastination. Push yourself to stay on point and watch yourself perform amazing feats.

Work-Life Balance

You've probably heard this familiar quote: "All work and no play make Jack a dull boy." Without time off from work, a person becomes both bored and boring. The exact origin of the phrase is unclear, though it was recorded as early as 1659.

This statement rings true when it comes to work and non-work-related activities. As you move toward your goals, it is essential to devote time to your family first. Family comes first, and there must be a harmonious balance between your family, personal, and work life. Know when to put your work aside and make time for yourself and things you enjoy. This is essential for good physical, emotional, and mental health.

Your family needs you to be present in mind and spirit. When you are with your family, let them know you are there by giving them your attention. Maintain quality in the relationships you have with the people who are closest to you.

Work has a way of taking your focus away from the people you love. Do your best to establish boundaries and set specific times where you will step away—and not do any work. Stay diligent about these rules you set for yourself. When you are away—you are away. When you are at work—you are at work. When you employ this in your life and establish the boundaries, you will find a much improved personal and family life; along with significant improvements within your work life.

Be Yourself All the Time

We are all unique. Perhaps in your life, you have modeled yourself after someone else you admire. Maybe your actions mimicked their actions. Was it a positive experience? Was it a negative experience for you?

Learning who you are as you, your strengths, and your weaknesses, is essential in achieving what it is you really want to see, experience, and remember. Being yourself and understanding who you are, while remaining steadfast in your individuality, is vital.

Being yourself and staying true to who you are is the key to a successful and rewarding career and enjoyable life. Never try to be like someone else—it is an impossible feat. There isn't anyone like you because we are all distinct with unique characteristics that make us who we are. Be yourself and love yourself all the time and remain steadfast in who you are.

Bend...Do Not Break

One of Aesop's fables, "The Oak and the Reed," describes a big tree and some thin grasses during a windstorm. The oak was pushed to the ground by the strong wind, but the grasses thrived. The oak could not bend like the grasses and it broke.

I have heard similar words in a song. I thought they were meaningful in many ways. The lyrics are from "That's What Makes the World Go Round," a song composed by Richard and Robert Sherman in the movie "Sword in the he Stone." Here is the link to a video of the song: at (youtube.com/watch?v=TegT074LKrw).

In my mind, when it comes to looking at our lives, these words ring true. Life is filled with opposites. You, along with each of us, are going to have issues in your life which could knock you down and take you off course. When you get knocked down, you must learn to get back up and face the challenges ahead. This is what I like to refer to as "bending like a reed but not breaking."

Knowing the person that you are and the value you bring to the table will help you to get back up to your feet. You must know your strengths and use them to get your life back on course. I encourage you to begin understanding your capabilities and relying on your specific strengths to help you persevere against any time of trouble in your life. When you are down, that is the time to dig deep and show the world what you are made of.

Although you don't have to prove anything to anyone, you need to directly hit adversity with all that you are made of—to get your life back. Facing major dilemmas and hitting them head-on is admirable, respectable, and builds strong character inside and out. One thing I know is you should never quit. Never give up during the storms of your life. Take the issues at hand, learn from them, deal with them, and move on. You can overcome anything in front of you with inner-strength and the desire to persevere. When life hits hard—bend like a reed. You can't ever break—you are too strong for that.

Why to Let Go of Toxic Negativity

As you go through life, from youth to adulthood, you will endure adverse experiences and negative people. When someone is negative it does not necessarily mean that person is terrible. Negativity can be anything unhelpful, pessimistic, and or destructive. I'm also talking about people, who from their personalities, have had a negative influence on your life. It could be a boss, a neighbor, or more than one person in any of your circles.

It could be a group of friends who cause stress and negativity for you.

If you stay around negative people, it will rub off on you. It will influence your behavior and change things for the worse. Even people who think negatively can project negative thoughts, which can be detrimental to you achieving goals and moving forward in your life. The people you associate with and surround yourself with mold you into who you were, who you are, and who you will become. When you are around negative people, you will get negative results. Positive people bring positive results. Negativity is not healthy and is even toxic. I've had many people in my life who were toxic, and I knew it. I had to make hard decisions and break ties with these people, and it wasn't easy.

In these types of relationships, use your best judgment about the people around you. Be honest with yourself; if you feel toxicity and bad things from listening or being around certain people, distance yourself from them. Get away from the toxic negativity and watch your life improve. Listen to what people say. Listen intently to their attitude. Is their demeanor made up of negative thoughts or actions? You will be the judge about what feels right and what is right for you.

As you control the negative situation, you alone have the choice to stay or leave. When you are confronted with this type of decision, whatever it is, you need to make an executive decision to be the leader of your own life.

Be honest. Is the situation good or bad for you? If it is acceptable, then let the relationship continue, but if it's not right for you—get out of it as quick as you can. Toxicity hangs on and becomes difficult to remove the longer it is present. Search yourself and listen to your feelings. If things aren't right—move on.

Have the Goal to Have Fun

Life has its ups and downs and challenges. However, life doesn't have to be all work; it can be enjoyable and fun. It is all up to you and how you approach every aspect of your life. Choosing to relax, to take time off and follow your passions are what makes your world (and the whole world) a better place. Make it a goal to find your passion and go after it. Ask yourself what you love to do. What is that one thing that you are great at doing? Finding a passion that inspires you is time well spent—acting on that passion is time better spent.

Once you find your passion set a goal to pursue it with everything you have. Most people don't explore themselves or their capabilities. I've seen many people not truly understanding who they are. And I've witnessed people spending their lives searching for something that is already within them—if only they had taken the time to stop and recognize. Most people settle for less, only to get by.

When you find this place in your life where you are doing the one thing you love, happiness and joy will surround you and fill you up. Success is great, and I am behind you in finding great success in whatever you choose to do. But, understand that success doesn't mean happiness. You can be successful and miserable at the same time. You may be good at something, and it brings wealth, security, and notoriety, but it could be something you hate to do.

Being miserable is painful and not enjoyable. Find your talent and pursue it with all that you have. Go after it; find joy and happiness, along with peace. Know you are doing what you love. Most people don't know their talent or ignore what is important to them only to settle for making money and working all the time in a job they don't enjoy. By following this path, at some point, you become miserable and possibly give up on anything else by continually doing what you don't like to do.

There is a quote from Steve Jobs that brings this into perspective: "If you don't love it, you're going to fail." Find your passion, your love, your drive, and get busy doing that. This will lead to having joy and happiness in all aspects of your life. Find and make time to pursue your passion and make that an essential goal within your life.

Mistakes Are a Path to Future Success

From the minute you were born, you were meant to make mistakes. Mistakes are the ingredients of life that shape and mold you into the person you are. Experiences form your personality, your goals, and your passions.

The way to embrace what feels like a mistake is to learn what you did wrong, how things went wrong around you, assess how you can never repeat that mistake, and set a goal to never fall victim to making a mistake again. Disaster happens if you keep returning to the wrong decisions and making the same mistake. Repeated mistakes turn into ruins for relationships, family life, even your leisure time, and always for your career.

Knowing how you learn from mistakes is the way to improve your life. Making mistakes is the fastest way you will discover things about yourself. How are you ever going to know the real "you" if you haven't fallen down a time or two? When a baby tries to walk, they fall. But they get back up and try again and again until they eventually walk. If a baby can learn how to get back up from falling, you can too. When you find yourself down, pick yourself back up, try harder, and get back living your life. This is the key to having a prosperous life. Learning from mistakes, trials, errors, and improving yourself from what you gleaned is the way.

Everyone deserves a second chance, and just because you've made a mistake doesn't mean there aren't options. No error is terrible if you put it in the right perspective. When you use what you learn, and apply the information toward improving, the next outcome forces the mistake to become an opportunity.

Mistakes are milestones and opportunities to learn. So, if you are not falling and making mistakes, you are not moving forward. You need to move forward in your life and do your best not to make mistakes; however, slipups can be a positive aspect for you along the way.

Your Time is Precious

When I was growing up, I learned to set goals to improve my life from an early age. My brothers pushed me, and I forced myself to obtain the things in my life I needed and wanted. It wasn't always easy. There was struggle, pain, and confusion, but I did not let it stop me or get me down. I learned from my failures, improved upon what I learned to make my life the best it could be. I worked hard and pushed myself to meet every challenge set before me.

You have the same choices—to work hard, set goals, and follow your passion. Set daily, monthly, weekly, and long-term goals. Decide and make sure that the plan includes your desires and what you love to do. Most of all, follow the path your heart takes you on, and if you stumble—get back up, learn from your mistakes, and carry on.

None of us are promised tomorrow—but life without goals is an empty life. Your goals over time will vary so learn to include them as parts of your relationships and family, work and careers, hobbies, and health. These are essential things in your life. Take each day as a fresh start and a new beginning. Remember that number: 86,400 seconds in a day. No more and no less. Use those seconds to the fullest, experience life, face challenges, embrace happiness and choose a path that will lead you to the life you desire. Do not take your days for granted, as each day is a gift from God. Life happens by squeezing the riches out of every second and following your dreams. Go and make your magic happen.

Don't hold onto things you can't control. Give God the first place in your life."

Quiz: Your Time Management Profile

How to use this quiz: Get a sheet of paper or use a computer and create a blank document. Write the date at the top of the page. Read each question on the list and evaluate which ones you feel most compelled to answer. Write out those questions you feel are most important, and then write your answers. Keep the document in your planner or in a place where you can see it daily. Each time you read over it for self-counseling, mark the date so you can track your progress. At the end of a week—whether or not you feel you've made progress—come back to this quiz again and re-take it. It is meant as a tool to measure your use of the 604,800 seconds you used in a week of your life!

1. Is it essential to set goals for your life at this time? Why or why not?
2. What are your current goals?
3. Goal setting has multiple benefits—what benefits do you see right now?
4. How would you rate your current level of procrastination?
5. How would you rate your current level of laziness?
6. How do you rate your current use of social media and other outlets?
7. How has your use of social media caused procrastination and distraction?
8. What is your best method for prioritization of tasks?
9. In what areas of your life do you want to eliminate clutter?
10. What bad habits have you formed through routine?
11. What good habits have you formed through routine?
12. What are common causes of disruption in the routines you've planned and desire to keep?
13. How do you take breaks from work for relaxation?
14. What was your most recent success in efficiency and productivity on a project or goal?
15. How do you materialize a goal through vision?
16. How do you materialize a goal through direct action?
17. Is your work-leisure routine in good balance?

After completion of this exercise, review the chapters in this book. Which one should you re-read for direction right now?

Answer key: Your answers to this quiz are relevant for the moment in time when you took the quiz. They may change over time. When you feel that you are off your desire track, come back to these questions and reassess your issues to re-gain a direction that feels better, that feels right to you.

My goal is for you, after you've read this book, is to live a peaceful, prosperous life and to give you tools to let you fashion such a life.

Acknowledgments

Having written this book, I see there are many people who deserve my thanks. First, I thank God for giving me the opportunity, the passion, and all the beautiful blessings of my life.

I specially dedicate this book to my aunt, Rose Marie Belizaire. She passed away in 2017, but she taught me everything I know today through examples and lessons. She used many social opportunities to instill etiquette and good manners in me. What she taught me became a permanent part of my life, from childhood into adolescence and beyond. Aunt Rose pushed me intellectually; she always reminded me never to stop learning, and to go as far as possible in terms of education. I took her advice to heart and followed. For that, I will always love you, auntie!

Made in the USA
Las Vegas, NV
24 December 2021